Woodrow Wilson
at Princeton

Woodrow Wilson as president of Princeton University.

WOODROW WILSON AT PRINCETON

by Hardin Craig

NORMAN
UNIVERSITY OF OKLAHOMA PRESS

LIBRARY OF CONGRESS CATALOG CARD NUMBER: 60–7738

COPYRIGHT 1960 BY THE UNIVERSITY OF OKLAHOMA PRESS,
PUBLISHING DIVISION OF THE UNIVERSITY.
COMPOSED AND PRINTED AT NORMAN, OKLAHOMA, U.S.A.,
BY THE UNIVERSITY OF OKLAHOMA PRESS.
FIRST EDITION.

To the Memory of Stockton Axson

Contents

Illustrations

Preface

THE PURPOSE OF THIS BOOK is to identify and explain Woodrow Wilson's opinions and principles in the field of university education. In order to do this clearly, it has been necessary to describe the actual situations in which they found expression. Underlying this discussion, is the idea that these opinions and principles are still alive and applicable in American universities. Indeed, it may be only incidental that the issue arose at Princeton rather than in some other university. It is even possible that the greatness and sincerity of Princeton caused them to manifest themselves there rather than elsewhere. It is obvious that I could not and would not use the great institutions with which I have been connected for considerable periods—Minnesota, Iowa, Stanford, North Carolina, and Missouri—as immediate objects of comparison. I can only proceed on the basis of a general concept of American university education, leaving special applications of Wilson's ideals and operations to those whose business it is to make them. The problems as I see them are quite general, so that in presenting Wilson as a leader in the field of higher education, I have trusted the clarity of my own recollections and my own loyalty to make what I have to say both just and objective.

In some matters, at least, I think I have rendered a service to knowledge and truth. I have, for example, attempted to make it clear that the Princeton over which Wilson presided was already a great, generous, and competent institution of higher learning. The reforms instituted were improvements or attempted improvements not only of Princeton but of American universities in general. I have also attempted to view the whole movement in terms of a great philosophy inherited by Wilson and his colleagues from James McCosh, a philosophy, moreover, that has been restored to vitality by the findings of the greatest group of scientists and philosophers of our present-day. Finally, as a matter both of justice and of sincerity, I have tried to remove from my account every trace of partisanship.

And now, there is the matter of acknowledgments. I should like to express my sincere gratitude to the Woodrow Wilson Foundation for financial assistance in the preparation of this book. I should also like to thank the personnel of the Princeton University Library, as well as the Alumni Records Office of the Johns Hopkins University, for their kindness in supplying me with photographs and giving me permission to use them. And last, but certainly not least, I am appreciative of the right granted me by Doubleday and Company to publish extracts from Ray Stannard Baker's *Woodrow Wilson: Life and Letters* (8 vols., New York, 1927–39).

Hardin Craig

COLUMBIA, MISSOURI
JANUARY 3, 1960

Woodrow Wilson
at Princeton

CHAPTER I

The Reformer

Woodrow Wilson returned to Princeton University, his alma mater, in 1890, as a member of its political science faculty. The substantial number of his addresses, articles, and letters already published at that time attest to his already definite opinions regarding the purpose of education and the proper means of accomplishing it. As president of Princeton from 1902 to 1910, Wilson saw that Princeton and other American universities of his time, with their emphasis on specialization and the new scientific methods, were not producing the dedicated leaders necessary to the preservation of the nation's democracy. He consequently utilized his great leadership, wisdom, and ability for the purpose of recasting university education at Princeton, his principal goals being breadth in each individual field of study and intimate relations between teachers and pupils in the preceptorial system (a sort of tutorial system). I was a postgraduate student and instructor for four years under Francis Landey Patton, Wilson's predecessor in the presidency of Princeton, and was a member of the Princeton faculty throughout Wilson's revolutionary administration. I was thus associated with Wilson's reforms but knew well the Princeton that was reformed.

Before I record my own Princeton experience, I feel it

necessary to review Woodrow Wilson's earlier career and discover, as best I can, the ideas and opinions about education that he inherited and developed. Material is extremely abundant, and no man was better than he at making himself understood. His career is an open book, and I make no claim to any advantage of special intimacy or personal knowledge. To read about Wilson's earlier life has helped me to interpret my own recollections and to treat more adequately the subject in which my interest lies. Principally I have used the first two volumes of Ray Stannard Baker's *Woodrow Wilson: Life and Letters,* which is full, intimate, and reliable, with some other biographies and memoirs and naturally a substantial number of Wilson's addresses on educational subjects. My interests have been satisfied with simple illustrations, and I have no theories about Wilson as a man, much less as governor, president, and world leader, to explain and justify. In that connection I am merely an American citizen, and in my busy life as a university teacher I am possibly less well informed than many others. I merely wish to find out why Wilson said what he said and did what he did as a university professor and administrator.

When I look back on the great leader who influenced my early years as a university student and teacher and try to determine the greatest single idea held and enforced (as much as might be) by Woodrow Wilson, I come to a very simple conclusion. It is that in the educational process Wilson believed in learning rather than teaching. He was not, perhaps, a man of highly complex character, but he was a clear-headed man of great and insistent force. This power he put behind ideas. From it may have come his well-known and slightly boastful statement that he was possessed of a "one-track mind." He was, nevertheless, within his own ample field a man of broad and accurate learning. By taste and conviction he had devoted his keen intellect to the field of political history, and it is absurd for any of his critics to question either his determination to find truth or his competency in finding it. This hangs together with the fact that he had more than his share of human charity and not only consideration for his fellow men but deep faith in their essential rectitude and their capacity for thought as well as action. It is as if he had anticipated the quite recent physiological belief that the human brain, however far it may usually fall short of its possibilities, is capable of developing three billion synaptic connections or separate ideational events. His belief in the intellectual possibilities of man perhaps stemmed from his acceptance of the teachings of Locke, Rousseau, Jefferson, and Bagehot. Wilson was not hasty or partisan in the adoption and development of ideas and beliefs, but, when he had adopted them, they became part of him and strode forward with him towards realization. His attitude was positive, so that he dwelt on the three billion possibilities rather than on the meager three million said to be repeated and manipulated by practical men.

To believe in intellect among all men is to allot a just portion to oneself. From this statement might be derived a definition of individualism, and a history of renascence, big and little, would furnish illustration. Granted that these natural powers are usually dormant and in early manhood often already decadent, the fact remains that it is normally absurd to resort to other people's brains instead of one's own and to put faith in teaching rather than in learning. Native powers manifest themselves under such pleasant epithets as "great," "inspired," and "creative." Particularly, the word "genius" has been given an unscientific definition and has been ruined by a mystical disguise. The possession of genius is considered a matter of divine revelation, an indefinable thing called inspiration or intuition, or in the whimsicality of existence, a mere matter of luck. It must reside within the brain and be the development of innate powers originating in the multifarious experience of the human animal on earth. This idea, if true, would be a sound basis for a theory and policy of education. It is significant in this connection that Wilson adopted and used Bagehot's conception that genius is the possession of ordinary powers to an extraordinary degree. As if in answer to conceited little persons who regard themselves as superhuman, Wilson was careful to remark that the degree of human ability might be as great as anyone was able to conceive. Learning was thus the natural approach of the individual to the problems and enterprises of life, whereas teaching was often the reliance of those whose satisfaction with the social and political *status quo* was such that they wished that they and their offspring might continue to live on the sunny side of the best of all possible worlds. One may pause long enough to express surprise and some dismay before the fact that teaching and not learning is the educational mode and reliance of the American people—so many years, so many courses, so many credits.

Wilson struggled with this question, and on more than one occasion that I remember, it took this form. He said that much instruction went into one of the student's ears and out the other. He said that nothing was done with the fact or idea while it was, so to speak, inside. No connections were made between the new idea and ideas already resident in the recipient mind, and no thought or action resulted from the experience. He acknowledged ironically that the current practice of conveying bodies of information to students and compelling them to pour it out in written examinations was an act of intellect, but declared that he regarded it as the lowest form of intellection. Wilson, himself a brilliant lecturer, nevertheless distrusted lectures as a means of education. Information, he thought, should come from books and experience. I remember that at a meeting of the faculty

6

of my department he explained very clearly what he thought the function of academic lectures was. He said that they were useful and economical of time when devoted to synopses and epitomes of subjects, since by their means students might grasp quickly and clearly parts, divisions, and aspects, and thus find their way about in an area under consideration or about to be studied in detail. A second use of lectures was what he spoke of as "trial trips" or demonstrations of method. On such occasions, he thought, a lecturer might carry out before his college audience a definitive piece of research or operative exposition in order that it might serve as a pattern of procedure. He did admit rather grudgingly that some lectures might, on occasion, serve to awaken interest and stir students to enthusiasm and effort.

Always, it seemed to me, Wilson's faith resided almost solely in what the student might do for himself. To this view, in spite of American practice, there can be no reasonable objection, and, as will be seen later, when Wilson made his greatest and best-known effort to reform university education, it was in line with this principle. Teaching, to him, was a matter of advice and guidance by those more mature and experienced in fields of human learning for those less so, and was therefore a matter of intellectual companionship and joint participation in the pursuit of learning in its various aspects. In this "discussion" or "meeting of minds," in this association in intellectual processes, Wilson placed lifelong reliance. The best illustration I can give is an experience of my own.

In the Princeton that Wilson attended, the two ancient literary or debating societies were great factors in student life. They rested on student interest in public affairs and were self-directed. They seemed to him educationally right and important. Interest in debating had declined with the years, however, and I was the agent and he the inspiring and directing force in an attempt to revive debating in the American Whig Society. The experiment was, strictly speaking, done in a corner. It attracted little interest and awoke no hope in the university of those days. University teachers are not often greatly interested in undertakings in which they themselves are not involved. For a period of about four years at the end of Wilson's administration as president of the university, I planned, directed, and encouraged activities in debate and public speaking in Whig Hall, and restored, as well as I could, the free and voluntary conditions that had existed at an earlier day. Wilson's interest did not flag. He visited us often and expressed to the students many times his faith in debating as a developmental force in education. I recall that he gave accounts of exciting or amusing debates in which he had taken part or which he had heard when he was an undergraduate member of the society. He rarely failed to reveal his keen interest in the maneuvering subtleties of parliamentary practice. After his departure, Princeton, no doubt quite properly, formalized and departmentalized the project and thus destroyed such spontaneity as we had been able to awaken. Yet I cannot say that this experiment in largely self-directed training, although relatively unimportant, was a failure, for I recall half a dozen or more men who are now rather important at the bar, in the pulpit, or in public life who worked zealously in my groups. College students are perhaps not so difficult to lead as we sometimes think they are. The point is that Woodrow Wilson, in the midst of his overwhelmingly busy, extremely responsible, and none too placid career as president of Princeton University, found time to interest himself in public speaking and debate. It must be remembered that his interest rested on his faith in self-directed, spontaneous intellectual activity on the part of students themselves.

My own long and consciously directed experience denies

8

the belief that truth always emerges from discussion and debate. I know the general use of disputation as a teaching method in the Middle Ages and the Renaissance and have no desire to discredit it, but the teachers who taught me most and inspired me to explore new fields and increase the range of my knowledge and interest did not follow a discussion method. C. H. A. Wager, Bliss Perry, John M. Manly, and A. S. Napier were not interrupted by banal, self-conceited queries and opinions. Their students saw without diversion great minds at work in the presentation of fact transmuted before their faces into systematic truth. I have been bored, therefore, with panels and conferences. I totally reject the idea that when a group of persons, none of whom knows anything definite about a subject, meet together to talk and dispute, truth will somehow emerge. Truth is not that easy to find, and I feel sure that the goddess of truth will, for her own peace of mind, absent herself from such welters of triviality, irrelevance, and egotism. Certainly Wilson had no such silliness in mind. He did believe that there is something vital and important in the meeting, even the clash, of minds, but these minds must be informed and sincere.

Before proceeding further, let us look more carefully at Wilson's principles of education as revealed in his career and in his marvelously clear statements.

He was brought up to hold a firm, yet unsentimental, belief in the Christian religion. The religious opinions he held have been called, sometimes derogatorily, Calvinistic, and this is correct. Yet one must understand that Calvin was not, in all senses, a Calvinist. Oddly enough, Francis Landey Patton was a great expositor of Wilson's religious views. He defined Calvinism as a great system of thought devoted to the concept of God's relation to the universe, which was, for example, ready to accept the findings of science as revelatory of the activities of an actual creator and ruler of the universe. This is the only creed, he thought, that is willing for God to be what He is. More specifically, Wilson was brought up in the Presbyterian church of the South. This institution, still intellectually aligned at that time with the Presbyterianism of Scotland, believed in education and therefore in intelligence. It had been conspicuous in the founding of institutions of higher learning in this country and had contributed much to principles of individual and political liberty in the establishment of the United States of America.

More particularly still, Wilson belonged to a southern group conspicuous for learning and scholarship. His father, Joseph R. Wilson, whom I remember very well, was a man of power, distinction, and intellectual eminence. Wilson's maternal grandfather, Thomas Woodrow, was a man of recognized scholarly importance. There were others, family friends, relatives, and associates, who were intellectual leaders in their communities and region. These facts will soon become significant. These men in Wilson's early environment were all theologians, and later there will be occasion to explain the epistemology they knew and used. With this background, one may say that Wilson, since he did not enter the ministry, devoted himself quite earnestly to the service of God, or, since the two are identical in the New Testament, to the service of his fellow men. Without forgetting the broader principles, he narrowed his mission still further and avowedly devoted himself to the service and salvation of the nation. "I try," he says, "to join the function of the University to the great function of national life," or, as Baker puts it, "The chief end of life" is "to discipline men to serve the state, religiously, loyally."[1]

From the beliefs and principles not unique with Wilson but firmly accepted and pursued by him, I think I should

[1] Ray Stannard Baker, *Woodrow Wilson, Life and Letters* (8 vols., New York, 1927–39), I, 183 ff., 212; II, 1 ff.

first select *order,* a word of general application that needs definition to render it significant. I recall my impression as a student that he believed in reformation as regards the political institutions under which we live and the customs and practices of statesmanship, but that he wanted no revolutions. He regarded American democracy as a gradual growth towards the order and harmony tried and tested by the experience of Englishmen for five hundred years or more and by Americans for a shorter but equally intense and important period. It is easy to pigeonhole this attitude and blur its significance by calling it conservatism, but there is more to it than just that word with its narrow connotations. What Wilson believed should be conserved was tested political experience and an intelligent conception of God and His service. Therefore he saw no reason at all for recasting the Constitution of the United States and the system of religious belief in which he had been brought up. Both, he thought, might be amended in such a way as to restore their fundamental principles to efficacy in an age that no longer understood and applied them. This doctrine is thus readily translated into ordering or adjustment, which is the active aspect of the political, moral, and religious system that our people have developed and adopted by their experience. Thus Wilson may well be classified as a reformer.

Back of a sense of order there must be a sense of unity in human existence and in the universe itself. That, too, Wilson had. "History," he said, "is past politics and politics present history." This is an important fact, for from it comes an epistemology that derives truth immediately by means of the completest possible comprehension of event or situation, a comprehension so complete that it reveals immediately agreement or consistency of parts with one another and with the generalized conception of truth.

It was thus inevitable that Wilson should have developed

the habit of hard study and that that study should have been followed by clarity of concepts and immediate and efficient action. Concerning this matter of order, it is interesting to remember Wilson's special absorption with constitutions and his tendency to establish systems and orderly institutions. "I have," he declares, "a sense of power in dealing with men collectively which I do not feel always in dealing with them singly. In the former case the pride of reserve does not stand so much in my way as it does in the latter. One feels no sacrifice of pride necessary in courting the favor of an assembly of men such as he would have to make in seeking to please one man."[2] Wilson's constitution for the "Wesleyan House of Commons" still exists, and in it will be noted his demand for sincerity on the part of debaters. Wilson disliked the advocate's boasted ability to speak on any side of any question, and I have heard him stress both sound information and honest advocacy of right before debating groups in Whig Hall. Wilson's belief in order was, I think, based on the perdurable nature of principle.

He saw the necessity for proper social organization if peace and progress are to be achieved, but how is this organization to be created and maintained? His belief in justice and his recognition of the doctrine of the consent of the governed put the answer somewhere in the area of established principle and make it an affair of the mass of men rather than of the individual. There is no great mystery here. Wilson's recognized youthful authorities were principally Edmund Burke, John Bright, Walter Bagehot, and to some degree Hamilton and Jefferson. These men he approached with proper humility, and their precepts go a long way in accounting for his accepted political principles. But it was the development of individual power that he most ardently sought. Even then he could declare, "The penalty for cramming one's mind

2 *Ibid.*, I, 199, 303.

with other men's thoughts is to have no thoughts of one's own."[3] I can still hear Woodrow Wilson justifying popular government and explaining, in his masterly way, its proper workings. I recall that he rejected exclusiveness in suffrage, particularly the idea that only the educated and cultivated are competent to pass on political issues. This he did on the ground that all sane men, having merely lived and met the issues of living, are able to judge between right and wrong, advantage and disadvantage, widsom and folly; in fact, that they judge these things extremely well. I cannot quote his words or remember the points of his argument. I can only record the enduring impression made on me by his teachings. My memory does record instances of his simplicity and naturalness in contacts with poorly educated people. The impression made on me was one of sincerity, as if he had taken to heart his own doctrine of man's relation to man. When he became a candidate for public office in 1910, voters were surprised by his lack of the least trace of condescension.

I think I am safe in summing up what I learned from Wilson in these terms: political freedom itself is not a single discovery, but a growth gradually made and tested by minorities throughout the ages, often discarded or forgotten, and even now threatening to become one of the lost arts. Wilson, I believe, so regarded it. I know that cultural evolution, like biological evolution, is a slow process proceeding through an infinite succession of trial and error. I learned from Wilson that it is only now and then, and at remote intervals, that men make beneficial discoveries in the field of government and that these discoveries are continually liable to be ignored or superseded by unworthy substitutes invented to serve some specious vanity or selfish interest. The great and lasting discovery of our race, Wilson believed, was liberty under the law, a sort of ordered individualism with its brood

[3] *Ibid.*, I, 87.

of civil blessings. I have felt that educated men should be leaders in the kind of reform, at once conservative and progressive, that consists in the restoration to greatness of the tradition handed down to us by our forefathers. I regard it as the only form of government that is in accordance with nature and civilization, and therefore as the only real government the world has yet seen. I have also the impression that the science of popular government is not, in its principles, an intricate matter, and that it has been made much more complicated than it really is. I look on complications not as exquisite adaptations of a system to its requirements, but as evidence of illness and decay. I think Wilson did so, too. This summarizes very roughly what the teachings of Woodrow Wilson meant to me. They concern us, because they do much to explain Wilson's belief that universities should devote themselves always, regardless of other obligations, to the wise and proper service of the state, a belief that runs all through his university career.

Granted the will to serve one's country and the belief in education to that end, how is one to reach the minds and hearts of the people, who are the responsible governors of a democracy; how is one to serve them well and assist them in securing faithful and intelligent servants? The business of government must go on in accordance with both justice and wisdom. It has seemed to me that Wilson's first reliance for means and methods was on what we would call communication—what his generation called oratory. His early career is full of oratory, debate, and discussion, and he never lost faith in the exact and adequate expression of truth. One of the current tenets of belief during both the Middle Ages and the Renaissance was that if the truth was clearly and exactly spoken, it had to be believed; hence the justification for the burning of heretics. If a heretic had had the truth made clear to him and had rejected it, it was proof that he was of and

14

from the devil and should be destroyed like the tares in the wheat. Of course, like jesting Pilate, one says, "What is truth?" But the matter is hardly as simple as that. If truth is an evolutionary factor, man's salvation has always rested on his recognition of it. There was no mysticism or fanaticism in Wilson's belief in the doctrine of the supremacy of truth. It is a perfectly tenable belief and, in his case, might have been inherited along with the Scottish philosophy in which he was trained.

It is obvious that this doctrine has even greater importance now than it did when he preached it. Suppose the state, or the states, should say, "We are willing to provide you with an opportunity to pursue higher education at our expense. We are not indifferent to your realization of such powers as you possess, because we think it important in a democracy that you should develop them to the fullest. But this is not the reason we pay your bills. We do it for our own good as political institutions, and, unless in your citizenship you make us a fair return, it is folly and waste for us to tax ourselves for your advantage." How does this honest statement agree with a system of education blatantly devoted to the specialized training of young men and women to serve their own special ends? These ends, it must be admitted, often comprehend the teaching of youth to prey upon society or, without one word about the rights and needs of society, the showing how one may get ahead of one's fellow Americans, in politics as well as business. Does it not seem foolish for the state to pay for the training of essential enemies? One might go further and ask why the state should harbor selfish interests in order that they may spread frivolity among its citizens and sell goods. These solipsistic forces might at least be made to pay for the privileges they enjoy. Selfishness has grown into a giant since Wilson's day, and although his idea that universities should serve the state is possibly dead, it is possible that, since it is sensible and prudent, it can be resurrected.

Whether or not there is any power in the tongue of man to induce Americans to serve and foster their great democracy, Wilson's early years are saturated with oratory. In an article in *The Princetonian* of June 7, 1877, he declares that oratory is not to be viewed as an end in itself but as a means, "its object persuasion and conviction in the control of other minds by a strange personal influence and power."[4] The means of acquiring this power was the imitation of classical models—Demosthenes, Cicero, Burke, Fox, Channing, and Webster. He speaks often of oratory as the art of persuasion and regrets that at the Hopkins style is neglected and ideas are everything. It is not therefore surprising to find him saying in maturer years, "The new school of economists revolt and say they want a more scientific method! What they really want is a higher literary method."

Wilson's quest for the exact word was notorious. He told me, and I think others, that he owed his training as a writer to his father. His father, he said, would ask him why he used one word rather than another and why he used certain words at all. I remember one occasion when he called me into his study to show me a letter from the late Professor John F. Genung, of Amherst College. In the most polite and appreciative way Professor Genung had asked permission to reprint a passage from *Mere Literature and Other Essays* as a model paragraph of rhetoric. Wilson granted permission but was puzzled and somewhat amused at the request. He said that he had never studied rhetoric and wondered how he could have complied in so exemplary a way with rhetorical principles. Of course, he knew very well how it had come about: perfection of form was in the nature of things, and he had taught himself. He never approved or saw the neces-

4 *Ibid.,* I 75, 104, 184.

16

sity of the formal teaching of English composition, which was then my job. He said that composition or style was to him a matter of the individual, differed from man to man, and was essentially an expression of self. It was on that occasion that he told me about his own experience. It was long ago and I was young, but I think even then I understood that he was gently instructing me.

I have always been uncertain about the nature of Wilson's faith in discussion. I can see that it may be a valuable device, but I think it needs to be both intelligent and sincere. Having devoted four years to the study and use of this discursive method, I am of the opinion that as a means of conveying information and encouraging the pursuit of learning, it is often ineffectual and time-wasting. It may fit men to carry their findings to audiences, but it is not the same thing as the pursuit of truth. It is recorded that from boyhood Wilson never read anything without wishing to discuss it fully. He continued the practice throughout his early years and no doubt as long as he lived. I recall being put on the spot when he asked my opinion about books and authors. This reliance on discussion is not hard to understand and justify. I merely question whether Wilson used it as a means of discovering and setting in order his own ideas and trying them out, or whether it was a manifestation of his inborn respect for the opinions of others. Perhaps it was the last mentioned. My experience points toward that conclusion.[5] Wilson talked over with me many of the issues that arose during his presidency of Princeton University. I was nobody, young and inexperienced, and he could have got little wisdom or assistance from me. Other men, I am sure, had the same experience.

Another very general principle believed in and followed by Wilson was the seeing and testing of ideas in practice.

[5] *Ibid.,* II, 110.

This is easily illustrated and from many points of view. The orator, he says, "must know the world of men and affairs."[6] Wilson followed persistently the political events in his own country and in foreign countries and read the best-informed journals as a matter of habit. His knowledge of history was not only intelligent but marvelously concrete. For me, this was one of his greatest charms as a lecturer. People spoke for themselves in his lectures and seemed alive, and events were real, echoes and all. Listen to this: "The whole proceeding impressed me as a shameless declaration of the determination on the part of a well-to-do community, to enjoy the easy position of a beneficiary of the national government to the fullest possible extent."

"The best way to learn things," he said, "is by direct contact." With this method should be associated a trained economy in the use of time. Baker hardly exaggerates when he asserts that Wilson never did anything twice.

Of the ideals Wilson particularly and persistently held, that of leadership was most important. I was puzzled by it during my days on his faculty at Princeton and by his famous dictum: "Princeton in the Nation's service." Of course, I saw its practical value and felt the inspiration of the challenge. I knew then and have observed during my years in the West, the Middle West, and the South that many leaders in our country have come and will continue to come, not from the halls of old, rich universities or from any universities at all, but from farms, small towns, slums, or where you will. The mere adoption by universities of a definite program of training and inspiring young men to become political leaders of a nation is excellent and noble, but it is not enough. The chances of such men for preferment to high political position are no doubt improved, but I think the sights were set too high. The ideal of making every Princeton graduate

6 *Ibid.*, I, 90, 151; II, 75.

an intelligent and responsible citizen seems to me more practicable and what all universities ought to strive to do for their graduates. I do not doubt that Wilson, who was a most perspicacious thinker, knew this well and provided for it in his conception of national benefit. I do not doubt that training and inspiring carefully chosen young men belonging to classes favored by surroundings of wealth and culture is a practical approach of great value, especially for the men so chosen, but it seems inadequate. Wilson himself taught that brains and character are not confined to the so-called better classes. The conception of leadership in our country must not be confined to presidents and generals of the army, or even to senators and governors of the states. Leadership needs to be integrated with our society and must be contented with a humbler role. It must, if our democracy is to be saved, appear in the home, the church, the neighborhood, and especially in business, not for the success of business but for the welfare of our country. I saw, and am sure that Wilson saw, that leadership must be moral and quantitatively immense. We must produce good, upright, intelligent, and patriotic men and women by the million in each generation, or we shall be on the rocks. Democracy is not a natural instinct of men—quite the contrary—and the doctrine of laissez faire is its ruin.

Wilson preached a doctrine of leadership, going, indeed, so far as to say that the training of political leaders was the chief duty and function of universities. In his own case, he regarded every other kind of achievement, teaching included, as a "secondary success." It is clear from Wilson's utterances that he regarded the teaching of leadership as a practicable undertaking, but I do not find it easy to determine just what he meant by leadership. In practice he stressed the necessity of students' knowing the operation of the government of the United States and the principles on which it was founded.

He made, moreover, many interesting statements about leadership, and inferences are possible. What he said concerns us all, especially those of us connected with universities.

At the very climax of his career as a world leader he said in an address in Paris, as recorded by Baker, "There is only one thing that can bind peoples together and that is a common devotion to right."[7] Here, perhaps, is the basis of Wilson's conception of leadership, for he believed in the invincible might of righteousness. Baker cites Wilson's early association with "highly cultivated people of strong character and clear ideas" and quotes from *When a Man Comes to Himself* a passage in which Wilson attributes to Christianity "the secret of social and individual well-being; for the two are not separable, and the man who receives and verifies that secret in his own living has discovered not only the best and only way to serve the world, but also the one happy way to satisfy himself."

Other statements are vague, but may have some bearing on leadership: "The young American when he gets to be an old American is going to be a useless American unless . . . he learns to use his mind."[8] This is in a letter to Charles Talcott, December 31, 1879, the year of Wilson's graduation from Princeton, when, according to Robert Bridges and other contemporaries, Wilson was already looked up to by his associates as a leader. Bridges writes, "We soon found out that he had an eager mind. That is a rare quality among youngsters of eighteen. But there was not a touch of the pedant or dig about him. He was as keen for the life of the college as any of us; but we soon discovered that what he called 'the play of the mind' was as exhilarating to him as the play of the body to the athlete. He took great pleasure in writers who used language with precision and imagina-

[7] *Ibid.,* I, xix.
[8] *Ibid.,* I, 88, 99; II, 102–103.

tion. To him this was not a scholastic pursuit. It was full of the stuff of existence. . . . This comradeship of his which began on this campus had a strong hold on him always. It included all kinds of men on the campus and diverse interests. He never lost the joy of it—and I know it often lightened his burdens."

The following from an oration of Wilson's published in *The University of Virginia Magazine* in 1880 is direct: "Absolute identity with one's cause is the first and great condition of successful leadership. It is that which makes the statesman's plans clear-cut and decisive, his purposes unhesitating—it is that which makes him a leader of states and a maker of history." This should also be added: "I want to keep close to the *practical* and the *practicable* in politics; my ambition is to add something to the *statesmanship* of the country, if that something be only thought."

There is also something substantial and direct to be derived from Wilson's essay, "A Calendar of Great Americans." The paper is full of wiredrawn distinctions among world figures: Hamilton and Madison, "great Englishmen bred in America"; John Adams and Calhoun, "great provincials"; Emerson and Asa Gray, "great authors and thinkers that might have been bred in any clime"; Jefferson and Benton, men of "mixed breed." Over against these are the real Americans, among whom he places Franklin, Jackson, Clay, and, at the top, Lincoln. In his analysis of Lincoln, Wilson enumerates qualities essential to the leadership of the American people: "Lincoln . . . never ceased to be a common man: that was his source of strength. But he was a common man with genius, a genius for things American, for insight into the common thought, for mastery of the fundamental things of politics that inhere in human nature and cast hardly more than their shadows on constitutions; for the practical niceties of affairs; for judging men and assessing arguments. . . . The whole country is summed up in him: the rude Western strength, tempered with shrewdness and a broad humane wit; the Eastern conservatism, regardful of law and devoted to fixed standards of duty. He even understood the South, as no other Northern man of his generation did. He respected, because he comprehended, though he could not hold, its view of the Constitution; he appreciated the inexorable compulsions of its past in respect of slavery; he would have secured it once more, and speedily if possible, in its right to self-government, when the fight was fought out. To the Eastern politicians he seemed like an accident; but to history he must seem like a providence."

Leadership begins to look like an aspect of American life to which American universities might well give attention. I had no choice; I had to study Wilson's doctrine of leadership as well as I could and adopt it in order to discharge my duty as a Princeton teacher. The conception we arrive at after reviewing it is definitely the moral basis of our republic and, we must believe, the only hope for the perpetuation of our system. How these principles appear in universities will be examined later. It will be observed that, except in some places and times, Wilson's reforms remain still to be carried out. As a whole, there is little evidence that American universities are following Wilson's lead. This is not his fault, but our attitude here is positive, not negative. This book does not dwell on the absorption of the greater number of American universities in materialistic ends. Reformation, I believe, is in the future, and I must confess that I rely more on the moral attitudes of all teachers and administrators than on oratory.

Wilson's ideas of university administration and government are analogous to those he held for states. In this connection one should read his article on "The Study of Administration," published in the *Political Science Quarterly* of

June, 1887.[9] This article seems to suggest in education, as in all great social undertakings, a confederation of parts rather than a centralization of power, and a wide union of tolerated divisions of prerogatives in pursuit of common purposes "in honorable equality and honorable subordination." In other words, educational institutions should assume a form and operation not unlike his ideal of the American system of government.

Wilson held other opinions which are significant in connection with his doctrine of leadership, since they are operative and may be conducive to success or liable to cause failure. No modern man was ever more inclusively ambitious than Wilson—for Princeton, for the nation, and for the world—but let it be understood that he expected effort and participation. The betterment he hoped for was not something that would just come about of itself. He thought he knew how to lead and how to establish reformation, and he had no intention of being a mere bystander.

From his school days in Columbia, South Carolina, he spent his time in dreaming and planning achievement.[10] He was critical of the education that was offered him and was disposed to think that he knew better than his masters what his education should be. Here begins the familiar tradition that Wilson "was not a brilliant student," a tradition that has, no doubt, brought great consolation to the idle and the inept, who seem never to have been told that, whether within the prescribed course of study or not, Wilson was notably industrious. He read widely and spent much time investigating social, commercial, and mechanical activities of all sorts. There is no doubt that he had a full share of the ardor

9 *The Public Papers of Woodrow Wilson, College and State* (ed. by Ray Stannard Baker and William E. Dodd) (6 vols., New York, 1925–27), I, 130–58.
10 *Life and Letters,* I, 58, 78, 103, 242.

and ingenuousness of youth. He is recorded as friendly, polite, enthusiastic, high in his aspiration, and genuinely interested in all kinds of human activities, including sports. He was not a selfish man, and I myself saw him undergo with comparative immunity the greatest of all dangers. I saw him live for years in an atmosphere thick with praise and within the sound of plaudits and shouts of approval. Nobody could have failed to be influenced by this, but he less so perhaps than almost anybody else on record. In saying this, I am aware of the basal assumption of Wilson's life, which was an avowed purpose of achievement. From the beginning, he was impelled to organize, inspire, and lead his fellow men. Granted this, Wilson is completely defensible. In dwelling on his ambition and his towering aspirations, one should not forget his concentrated effort. His effort was never *in vacuo* and was no search for mere self.

In an address before the High School Teachers Association, January 9, 1909, Wilson talks about writing and recalls the advice of his father: "Don't fire in such a way and with such a load that while you hit the thing you aim at you hit a lot of things in the neighborhood besides; but shoot with a single bullet and hit that one thing alone." This shooting with a single bullet is typical of Wilson in many things besides literary practice. It is an expression of what Baker calls Wilson's instinct for the main current[11] and was also characteristic of the philosophy and practice of James McCosh. It is closely connected with Wilson's belief in moments "when a man comes to himself," and is particularly exemplified in his wide miscellaneous reading. Every book he read had a special meaning that he was determined to comprehend. His approach to reading and writing is but another aspect of what Wilson himself spoke of as the necessity to "know the world." We shall have to reckon with those

11 *Ibid.,* 83, 86, 95.

self-conceited modern historians who measure Wilson with the yardstick of the scientific method and find him wanting, and shall return to this subject in discussing the epistemology in which Wilson was trained.

His objection to formalism in the educational process with his reservation of the right to industry and effort is certainly related not only to his doctrine of the necessity of direct action, but to his concept of the way the mind works. He learned early that the mind "is not a vessel to contain something," but "a vessel made to transmute something." The following passage from a letter of April 22, 1884, makes this clear: "The man who reads everything is like a man who eats everything: he can digest nothing; and the penalty for cramming one's mind with other men's thoughts is to have no thoughts of one's own. Only that which enables one to do his own thinking is of real value: which is my explanation of the fact that there are to be found in history so many great thinkers and great leaders who did little reading of books—if you reckon reading by volumes—but much reading of men and of their own times." Wilson sought in practice the independence of teachers—another of his roads to truth. A mature expression of his attitude is the following from his memorial essay on Dr. Adams in 1902:

His head was a veritable clearing house of ideas in the field of historical study, and no one ever seriously studied under him who did not get, in its most serviceable form, the modern ideals of work upon the sources; and not the ideals merely, but also a definite principle of concrete application in daily study. The thesis work done under him may fairly be said to have set the pace for university work in history throughout the United States.

This objective, irrespective of how it was understood and carried out, was basal to his educational plan, the preceptorial system of Princeton. Certainly the clearest quality of this plan, so far as it came from Wilson himself, was reliance on the independent use of the mind by the student himself. Wilson was from the beginning definitely critical of the formal educational processes of American universities, but the preceptorial plan underwent considerable modification in the direction of formal educational procedures. His ideal, not one that works well in the student life of our day since it provides for neither courtship nor athletics, is suggested by the following passage from an address before the Twentieth Century Club, January 3, 1903:

It is to get the spirits of men that the university is created; to my mind it is not to make scholars. No undergraduate can be made a scholar in four years . . . the very best effects of university life are wrought between six and nine o'clock in the evenings, when the professor has gone home, and minds meet minds, and a generating process takes place.

This is, of course, to reckon without the host and bears little relation to the conversation of present-day students in universities, but it points to the thing that Wilson found most valuable. The agency with its spirit is lacking. The spirit appears in the breadth of Wilson's views. He believed that his age was a new one, as we believe that our age is brand new, but he was never swept off his feet by new ideas and systems. There were, he thought, no absolutely new ideas,[12] no "successful new revolutions." There was only a steady, intelligent progress from the old to the new. For example, American history was "an integral portion of the general history of civilization; a free working out upon a clear field, indeed of selected forces generated long ago in England and the old European world, but no irregular invention, no his-

[12] *Ibid.*, II, 122, 129; I, 248.

trionic vindication of the Rights of Man." The new that he
saw in his age was mainly in the form of opportunity for
leadership. The elements were old. Wilson said many times
in many ways that education is not an end in itself. For him,
in his great belief in the all-importance of political institutions, education for all Americans should be education for
the nation's service. The principle held for all fields, but in
the universities with their specializations, no adjustment has
ever been made.

Another form of the conception appears in Wilson's dec-
larations that information is not education. This tiresome
and almost universally misunderstood commonplace receives some interpretation in Wilson's actions, if not in his
words. He even made the hazardous statement: "I want to
carry as little information in my head as possible," but added,
"I must *scan* information, must question it closely as to every
essential detail, in order that I may extract its meaning, but,
the meaning once mastered, the information is lumber."[13]
His very belief that the history of the United States "is an
integral portion of the general history of civilization" com-
mits him to illimitable knowledge and, let him struggle as
he might against it, he is already face to face with the para-
dox of scholarship, namely, that to know anything completely, it is necessary to know everything about it, even to
the frontiers of time and space. Meaning, which to him was
all important, is dependent on knowledge. It is interesting
in this connection to speculate on what Wilson's "Novum
Organon" of politics, projected but never written, would
have been like. I rather think that it would not have been
an encyclopedia, nor a logic, like Bacon's great work, but a
compendium of political theory.

Wilson's conviction that education, like democracy, is a
natural process or growth and not an invention is evident

13 *Ibid.,* I, 255, 271–76; II, 168.

in instances of what might be called his insight, as when he says, "You know that we hear a great deal of sentimental cant nowadays about cultivating our characters. God forbid that any man should spend his days thinking about his own character. . . . Your characters, gentlemen, are by-products and the minute you set yourselves to produce them you make useless prigs of yourselves." It appears also in Wilson's skill in the difficult task of raising the level of intellectual life among Princeton students. President Lowell of Harvard said, in commenting on Wilson's work as an educator, "He was also, as far as I am aware, the first head of a college who strove to raise the respect for scholarship among the undergraduate body." The division between matter and meaning probably explains Wilson's early prejudice against formal education in colleges and universities, a prejudice, by the way, that did not manifest itself during the considerable period of my service under Wilson at Princeton.

It was pointed out above that during his own formal education Wilson was a mediocre student but was conspicuously busy about his own intellectual ends. He even went so far as to say (an utterance largely contradicted by his own practice), "When you begin to be systematic, then you begin to depart from eternal verities, for eternal verities are not systematic," and he adds, "I found my text in the poets, who always come nearer real truth."[14] Axson, in a letter to Ray Stannard Baker, reports Wilson's saying this: "We who know literature by sight have the responsibility of carrying on a war with those to whom so-called 'scholarship' is everything."[15] I was perfectly familiar with this attitude, but I have never been able to see any necessary breach between scholarship and literary appreciation. In any case, this belittling of scholarship is a thing we shall have to work out,

14 *Ibid.*, II, 74; I, 229.
15 *Ibid.*, II, 101.

for it simply does not jibe with university education. In Wilson's case I do not think the impression is difficult to account for. The epistemology he had inherited, which had been reinforced by his Princeton training, was being superseded by the so-called scientific method, with its specialization and its Cartesian dichotomy between matter and spirit. This he found dry and ineffectual, as others did then and have since. His rebellion was intense, but he felt rather than understood the objections involved. Wilson was right, but he did not know why. This subject will be examined later, but meantime the extent of his dissatisfaction with the scientific method can be illustrated.

Wilson left the Hopkins with the doctor's degree practically in his grasp, the reason he gave for leaving without it being this: "I am quite sure that I shall profit more substantially from a line of reading of my own choosing, in the lines of my original work, than I should from much of the reading necessary in the Ph. D. course—though my *inclinations* will take me through most of that course." It will be remembered, however, that Wilson subsequently did take the degree. There is some significance in that fact, since it may be that with age and experience he outgrew his earlier beliefs. I think that none of us who worked under him at Princeton ever felt that he did not regard our subjects with sympathy and respect, and we saw him setting the *studium generale* in order and devoting his powers sincerely to the improvement of teaching. We should not have expected him to say, as he once did, "I have no patience for the tedious toil of what is known as 'research'; I have a passion for interpreting great thoughts to the world." There is a misunderstanding here. No knowledge, no great thoughts; Wilson knew this. The very idea of insight without knowledge is contradicted by his philosophy, his inborn desire to know, and his capacity and willingness to work. He never shirked a task. It may be that he discovered, as time went on, that there were other workers in the world besides him and even that there were other ends of learning besides history and politics.

There is also another contradiction that looms rather large, namely, Wilson's doctrine of thoroughness. The word echoes throughout his writings, and I think the reason why it does will become apparent. Wilson was one of the most careful readers on record. He mastered every book of whatever kind he read. As Baker says, he had a passion to know completely and accurately what an author had to say.[16] Wilson alludes to many books in his writing, usually by summary, but in his lectures he dictated page after page— my fingers ache when I remember it. He said in an address, "Great books have changed men's lives and altered the current of history." In the same address he explains why this is so: "I would not have you think that the writer of books is less steadily in search of reality than the builder of states or the conductor of great material enterprises or the man who is in the midst of action. . . . The man of letters has conceived his function too narrowly who does not see this." There is a quality of sincerity and a sense of the actual in his attitude towards recorded truth. Here, for example, is a practical statement of a situation: "I *can't* cram; I must eat slowly and assimilate, during intervals of rest and diversion. My chief ground of indictment against my professors here [the Hopkins] is that they give a man infinitely more than he can digest. If I were not discreet enough to refuse many of the things set before me, my mental digestion would soon be utterly ruined."

My recollection of the institution of the preceptorial system at Princeton confirms my belief that this idea of making haste slowly played no small part in Wilson's conception of

16 *Ibid.,* I, 86; II, 98; I, 216.

that more natural educational way. We have testimony also that the principle of thoroughness guided Wilson in his composition of *Congressional Government.* "The essay on the Senate," he says, "is not running so easily or so fast as it would were I feeling quite well; but every day sees some advance in it, and the slow laboured pace is doubtless friendly to *thoroughness.* I shall be quite satisfied if I can complete it by the end of this month."

What Baker says about the preparation of Wilson's second treatise on government, *The State,* is so characteristic and convincing that it is worth quoting:

It was a summer [1887] of hard work for Wilson, partly on the lectures for his Johns Hopkins course, chiefly on the German treatises in preparation for *The State.* He was indefatigable in the thoroughness of his method. An immense quantity of his notes, stenographic or written in his painstaking script, or on his typewriter, remained in his files at his death. At a time when the card catalogue method was in its infancy he employed it with great skill. He had a box of japanned tin which held cards 5x2 inches in size, and upon these he wrote his references, mostly in German and French, and part of his notes. Nothing could better reveal the care with which he studied the Greek and Roman systems, as well as the later development of the modern state. He spent three years of the hardest toil on the preparation of *The State.*[17]

This brings us to the end of an attempt to discover and list certain intellectual and moral qualities in Woodrow Wilson, qualities that seemed to his faculty significant and later influential, if not determinative, in his career as a university teacher and administrator. Interest has been restricted to that field. Attention has been called to Wilson's belief

[17] *Ibid.,* I, 285.

in the power of ideas, his intense and immediate desire to make ideas prevail, and to his faith in persuasion; to his faith also in the intellectual range and in the possibility of achievement of the individual human being. His conviction that the road to intellectual success lay through learning rather than teaching and that the formalization of educational practice hindered the individual and blocked his way has been pointed out. Although he distrusted the formal course, Wilson reserved to the student the right to work and found in discussion a sort of escape to individual proficiency in thought. Having an intense moral purpose towards better thoughts as well as better things and believing in the irresistible power of clearly uttered truth, he exploited the idea of leadership. An attempt was made to determine what Wilson meant by leadership, which he narrowed to a controlling extent to one field. Leadership was political, and politics was the nation's service. Because of its overwhelming importance in our country, the nation's service became the prime object of universities. An epistemological problem that concerns universities fundamentally was arrived at, with which this discussion has not finished, although the indications are that Wilson was right in accepting thoroughness of comprehension as the proper basis for the determination of truth. That he groaned over the labor in which his philosophy involved him but met it resolutely has been made clear. This account is of necessity incomplete, but may be useful. Synthesis of human beings is apt to be futile, especially when the human being considered is so varied in his interests, so vital and zestful as was Woodrow Wilson.

CHAPTER II

Pre-Reformation: Princeton, 1898-1902

I CAME TO Princeton in September, 1898, and entered the graduate school. I had been graduated from The Centre College of Kentucky in 1897 and had had what I have long recognized as a good college training, already slightly out-moded. I had fair fluency in Latin, was not bad in Greek and was rather keen about it, and had done well in mathematics through calculus. I had had brief courses in chemistry, physics, astronomy, geology, biology, psychology, ethics, and logic. Principally I had studied English under a great teacher, Charles Henry Adams Wager, afterwards a distinguished professor at Oberlin College. Older Oberlin men still respond cordially to Wager's praises. Why I came to Princeton I do not know.

The graduate school was in its infancy, mainly on paper, and modeled in its plans and standards on the German university. Andrew F. West was dean and W. F. Magie secretary. Magie took a somber view of the Princeton graduate school as an institution, and declared that things were in such a state that, if I made a proper degree, I should have to rely on myself. He appealed to me to do so. But Princeton was possibly better than he thought. Its very lack of regulations, tests, and compliances was a delight and, I think, a benefit to me. Nobody told me what courses to take, and I took an incredible number in an indefensible number of fields and pursued them with zeal. This went on for two years or more, and I recall that I studied Greek and Sanskrit, political science, the history of philsophy, European history, Indo-Germanic philology, German and Germanic philology, and other subjects now forgotten—all this in addition to Anglo-Saxon and Gothic, English literature, and some quite wonderful courses in poetics and prose fiction. The regimen was preposterous from any modern point of view but was delightful, and, since those were my acquisitive years, I think timely and ultimately beneficial. Princeton was a wonder world to me, and why not? I met some great teachers and great men, and I was, although I refused to admit it, from a border state not then distinguished for educational eminence. I brought enough pride of family and region to sustain me and at times to make of me something of a spectacle.

Princeton student life was almost exclusively undergraduate. It was, to say the least, obtrusive and dominant. It fascinated me, although I did not understand it well. Costumes in which orange and black cried aloud, parades and marching songs, with or without excuse, mild hazing, much informal participation in sports (Brokaw Field was relatively new), and innocent and rather polite gaiety were in order. There were still some riotous classrooms in which peculiar and helpless, rather than unpopular, college teachers were hazed. Woodrow Wilson, who of all men was in least danger of such treatment, told me that his worst dream was that he was in a classroom filled with shouting and disorderly students. I recall an undergraduate's being taken to task by some friends in the faculty for the current bad treatment of a newcomer in philosophy. The boy declared he had never done a thing in that class except laugh, and he couldn't help laughing because the teacher used repeatedly the funniest word he had ever heard. Asked what the word was, he replied, "Spinoza," which *is* a funny word.

Not having spent my undergraduate years at Princeton, I lack the certainty that might have come from personal experience and I have therefore talked the matter of the students over with some of my contemporaries. The conclusion is roughly this: The Princeton undergraduate body was not homogeneous, and this fact throws out easy generalizations. There were far more boys than one might suppose who came to college to get an education. They were not of wealthy or socially prominent families. They were in considerable numbers the sons of ministers and had great moral earnestness. Some worked their way through college. They were inconspicuous and quiet. They were not and did not expect to become athletic heroes.

They may perhaps be safely distinguished from a second type, the well-to-do who had come for the ride, to enjoy "bright college years," have a good time, and possibly get fame in sports and be regarded this side idolatry. They did not object to picking up the odds and ends of a liberal education provided it did not interfere too much with the main objectives. Indeed, many of them were much in earnest about getting an education and would be proud of their Princeton degrees, but the fact remains that those degrees depended mainly on cramming before examinations. They were, and those who survive still are, good fellows in the very best sense of that expression. In later years they tended to deprecate their study and to declare forgetfully that they "never cracked a book."

If "I. Q." ratings had been in existence, it is just possible that the second type would have ranked a little higher than the first, but that is conjecture. From both groups came brilliant architects, physicians, lawyers, preachers, politicians, and some scholars.

35

In numbers, the two types were about equal, with the group who were favored socially and financially slightly in the majority, and the two did not differ very greatly in their feelings and attitudes. The less favored group financially were just as intent on maintaining Princeton "traditions" as the other. Supporting the football team was *the* accepted enthusiasm, stimulated by calls for the "Princeton spirit." The boys in the bleachers on the occasion of the famous victory of 1899, the occasion of Poe's kick, were disposed to attribute the unexpected triumph over Yale to the fact that they themselves never lost heart, but on the call of the cheer-leaders continued to give series of nine mighty "locomotives," one after another. The elements of luck, nerve, and special skill were recognized, but the winning force was the spirit of the student body. One may look back on the football fervor with some amusement, it was so callow and exaggerated, but the whole community was involved—students, faculty, and alumni. In the autumn one lived in a football atmosphere. All other forms of athletics were informal, amateur, healthy, and sensible. I do not recall that any letter man was flunked out for low standing in studies. It may have happened, but the times were early and the unity was so complete that it allowed the claims of Princeton as an educational institution. I remember at least two heroes of the gridiron who worked hard to keep up their studies, considering it their public duty to do so.

There was a lot of convivial beer-drinking, but there was little conspicuous drunkenness in the student body. Younger alumni came back in an uncertain state and prowled the campus in a noisy but usually good-natured way. Sexual vice and gambling were at a minimum. There were occasional awed rumors about visits to a neighboring city, but the mode was easygoing, well mannered, and relatively moral.

In freshman and sophomore years few elective courses

were open, and those carefully supervised. They consisted mostly of choices between subjects, and the subjects were rather solidly introduced. No great opportunity for idleness is offered by a choice between chemistry and physics, for example. Not so the last two years. In them there were real opportunities for defeating the ends of serious study. Along with admirable advanced courses were electives of little substance, no system, and feeble standards. The group of less serious students tended to exploit this situation and actually established a fashion according to which it was bad form to elect courses that required work. They thus confirmed their idleness and increased their numbers. But even this was by no means universal. Many men who had been born with silver spoons in their mouths yielded to the lure of great teachers and great courses of instruction. Standards were not strict in any year, but they were eminently respectable in most areas. It was generally felt that Princeton was about right. It led an interesting and defensible life and tacitly accepted the idea that men of learning are necessarily a small and self-chosen few. In earlier days Princeton had not needed defensive tactics or recognized the fact that idleness and mere play hinder an institution of learning, spreading corruption among the young and inexperienced. It is an old issue and has been met in many ways in many institutions, or not met at all.

No faculty that contained Wilson, Winans, Ormond, Perry, Scott, Harper, and many others of like caliber may be ignored. Although none of us knew it, there was a job for that faculty to do in order to build Princeton up to its proper elevation, perhaps to restore to it, now much larger in size than in early years, an excellence equal to that it had once had. One need not take too seriously the banal boasting of the old grads, and yet it may be significant that too many of the alumni of those days looked upon Princeton merely as an opportunity for comradeship and sport, indeed, may have thought of those features as all that was required of institutions of higher learning.

Francis Landey Patton became president of the College of New Jersey (Princeton's name before 1896) in 1888, succeeding James McCosh, and resigned his position as president of Princeton University in 1902, when he was succeeded by Woodrow Wilson. That is the Princeton into which I blundered in September, 1898. The greatness of the McCosh administration and the brilliance of the educational reformation under Wilson have tended to overshadow or even denigrate the Patton period. Frankly, I think this is a mistake, for it was not the barren and shiftless time it has been said to be. Patton was a distinguished and congenial member of the McCosh faculty and was the best expositor of the McCosh philosophy in the university. It has sometimes been forgotten that during his administration enrollment greatly increased, but potent, though as yet undefined, social forces unsympathetic to educational ideals were in operation through no fault of Patton or anybody else. In Patton's later years, bitter opposition and frustration were in operation. Patton was not a reformer, but he had a choice to make, and we shall see what that choice was and the bases on which it rested. I merely suggest that it is only fair to look on the Patton administration as praiseworthy, but suffering from an inevitable defeat of the McCosh principles. There was an America at hand that demanded something not half so good. No one can deny that the Princeton of President Patton maintained under difficulties the greatness of the era of McCosh.

There were many mature scholars and excellent teachers in its faculty. After 1890, it had Wilson himself, whose influence was great and whose charm was compelling. For reasons that would not appeal to the modern world I took some

38

courses under him. I did not know very much, and simply and innocently wanted to know everything. Taking advantage of the lax regulations for graduate students, I studied widely, and the men whose courses of instruction I took were teachers and scholars of excellent quality. Wilson himself was one of the most sagacious and convincing thinkers I have ever heard talk. Bliss Perry in his distinguished Princeton days was giving lectures on poetry, prose fiction, and other literature. Alexander T. Ormond was a philosopher in his own right and a great teacher. I had Greek literature and Sanskrit under Samuel Ross Winans, whose reading of *The Odyssey* still lives in my memory and imagination. Edmund Yard Robbins was, in his quiet way, a revealer of the Greek spirit. O. H. Hoskins was a well-trained scholar. I had German philology under him, and Indo-Germanic philology under the brilliant Jesse Benedict Carter. And I shall not forget two of the older men, Dean James Ormsby Murray and Professor T. W. Hunt. Hunt had the rare quality of letting students read. Under him I read almost the entire body of Anglo-Saxon poetry with only casual interruption and comment. Late in my career as a graduate student, I derived great benefit from the investigative energy of Thomas Marc Parrott. There were other zealous teachers, many of whose lectures I heard in my free-lance career and so discovered the reason of their fame.

There was thus very little amiss, and that little, in its temporary aspects, was not hard to correct. But a larger view revealed difficulties, some of which could not be overcome except by long labor and the lapse of years. From this point of view it seems unjust (and political) to indulge the human habit of finding somebody to blame. Princeton had been growing, and growing from the patronage of the new commercial rich, a clientele often without an inheritance of education and culture. This is common enough, indeed a

familiar mode in American higher education. Lifting the
level of American learned culture is no child's play. We
make an effort and have some success along with a good deal
of frustration. The error lies in thinking we have succeeded.
There was no longer at Princeton, as in the days when Woodrow Wilson was an undergraduate, a preponderance of the
sons of ministers, doctors, lawyers, teachers, and old-fash-
ioned merchants. Too many of the newcomers, relieved of
the necessity of making their way in the world, preferred
idleness to work, and Princeton was a lovely spot in which
to loaf.

This paradise of leisure was, however, as has been pointed
out, in some measure restricted to the junior and senior
years. In the two lower years standards were to some extent
still in force, and, if freshmen and sophomores did not pass
their examinations, they were in danger of being sent home.
The classes disciplined one another a bit. It was considered
proper for freshmen and sophomores to keep up their studies,
and even quite idle juniors and seniors looked with real
contempt on underclassmen who neglected their studies and
were too gay, unless these underclassmen were promising
athletes, and even they were expected to keep out of trouble.
Most of the freshmen and sophomores actually did some
work; indeed, had some conscience about it. Some of them
engaged tutors to boost them over the barriers, and that situation suited me and my finances. I recall that one man,
later a benefactor of Princeton, had the thickest possible
head. Deep inside there were some brains, but it required
all my ingenuity to find a tortuous way of getting at them
until he was "safe now in the junior year." The work of
freshman and sophomore years had to be reckoned with, and
men like Fine, Thompson, and Westcott did something, at
least, to see to it. Princeton had not yet fallen into the great
American habit of mistaking riches and social position for

brains and did not yet worship notoriety and numbers. I saw little bootlicking of faculty by students, and I think the pitiful practice of teachers' flattering students was entirely absent.

Around the requirements of the two upper years there were many bypasses, not hard to find and not hazardous. They were well known, like those through the Hartz Mountains in the early days of the Iron Curtain. Such escapes are everywhere in all institutions and, if the administration is worth its salt, not hard to block. One type of escape is the "pipe" course, often taught by a tender-hearted old gentleman whose rascally students have persuaded him that the work offered is so difficult that the wind simply must be tempered to the shorn lambs (or black sheep). The professors who give these courses are gentlemen, needing only a quiet talk with a responsible official. The proud and self-respecting old professor, having learned that he is being looked down upon by his colleagues, will usually make adequate corrections and do so at once. Another bypass is opened by greedy, vain teachers who have fallen in love with large numbers in their classrooms, which they mistake for popularity. They present a more complex problem, the solutions of which are varied, but usually possible. It must be remembered also that the Princeton of those days was understaffed, as is the case in many American universities now. The lecture system had been imported from Germany and Scotland, and to it had been added the device of tests and quizzes. This enabled universities to get along, as they still do, with staffs that were too small. The free-elective system did the rest. But, all in all, it would take a great deal to convince me, in the light of my subsequent experience, that the Princeton of the period about which I am writing was not an excellent institution.

Princeton had a conscience, and the tenderness of that con-

science testified to the high quality of the men then responsible for the institution. I had no access to individual com-
plaints and little knowledge that they existed. Faculty discontent, so far as I was concerned, became openly manifest
in a series of faculty meetings in the second semester of 1901,
to which I shall later devote particular attention. Those were
the days before the hired-man conception of university instructors had established itself, and, through the thoughtful
generosity of the Princeton government, those of us who
were merely on temporary appointment were permitted to
attend meetings of the whole august faculty. To this day they
stand out in my memory as being among the greatest experiences of my academic career. The business of these meetings was to pass on the report of a committee appointed by
order of the faculty to investigate the scholastic standards of
the university and to make recommendations for reform.

Before I consider the Princeton situation in detail, however, I must lay a proper foundation. That foundation is
largely the teachings of James McCosh. It is ordinarily said
rather hastily that McCosh adhered to the principles of the
Scottish school of philosophy, and while this is true, it is not
the whole truth. These principles were nothing new to
Princeton and to learned Presbyterianism, Congregational-
ism, and other religious bodies of a Calvinistic creed in
America. But McCosh was a philosopher in his own right and
really advanced, purified, defended, and expounded in masterly fashion the system of philosophy known as the Scottish
school. He did this so effectively that he may properly be
ranked with Reid himself and would be, had it not been
that there had entered the field a victorious rival, to be considered farther on in this discussion. My tentative suggestion
is that the philosophy of McCosh is not dead.

This is commonplace. James McCosh was gifted with a
commanding personality, was a great and, through his ap-

42

peal to reason, dominant teacher, and was a man of altogether superior intellectual culture. He knew the sciences, was versed in literature ancient and modern (he was, for example, an excellent Greek scholar), knew his theology up one side and down the other, and was withal one of the world's greatest authorities on psychology, logic, and metaphysics. If anyone doubts this, let him read, first of all, that great book, *The Scottish Philosophy, Biographical, Expository, Critical, from Hutcheson to Hamilton* (1875). It opens, with wide learning, great insight, and profound importance, a lost world. It is lucid and extremely well written. and reveals the McCosh spirit, which is the spirit of the greatest scientists and philosophers of our most recent days. The book is critical without being destructive and controversial without a trace of partisanship. It is, for example, the severest critique of Hamilton's philosophy in existence and is, at the same time, the greatest tribute to Hamilton's genius. McCosh's success in his estimate of Hamilton and other philosophers throughout the book rests on the completest possible knowledge, a knowledge of amazing scope.

McCosh believed that the philosophy of a people, an age, or an institution is the most important thing about it. I, too, believe this commonplace and think it important on this occasion. I cannot do better than to follow his lead by repeating a paragraph from De Tocqueville's *Memoirs* which he quoted in the preface to the second edition of *An Examination of Mr. J. S. Mill's Philosophy; being a Defence of Fundamental Truth:*

The ages in which metaphysics have been most cultivated have in general been those in which men have been most raised above themselves. Indeed, though I care little for the study, I have always been struck by the influence which it has exercised over the things which seem least connected with it, and even over society in general. I do not think that any statesman ought to be indifferent as to whether the prevailing metaphysical opinions be materialistic or not. Condillac, I have no doubt, drove many people into materialism, who had never read his book; for abstract ideas, relating to human nature, penetrate at last, I know not how, into public morals.

Let us find out, if we can, the effect of McCosh's philosophy on Princeton (and possibly on Woodrow Wilson) and witness the impact of a hostile philosophy in an age of transition.

It looks as if the beginnings of modern university life as distinguished from college life made their appearance mainly in the administration of President McCosh. A postwar awakening was occurring in the greater institutions of the country. There was also under way an era of national prosperity. Harvard, Yale, Columbia, and Pennsylvania showed not only new life but expansion in the direction of science and technology. Cornell, Johns Hopkins, and Michigan were new institutions directed along the more liberal lines. At Princeton the new age began as soon as at any other college. It was led by McCosh and was definitely progressive. Its proponents did not go all out and make the common blunder of destroying the old on the appearance of the new. In this, one may well believe, they were right. A student of the Renaissance is not liable to forget that humanism included the whole *studium generale*—the seven liberal arts, the three philosophies, and many new subjects. The conclusion that because a man knows one thing, he cannot know another is a modern and largely American fallacy.

People of wealth, mainly alumni of Princeton, began making gifts and contributions to the university. New buildings were built, the faculty was increased in size and strength, and the College of New Jersey increased in enrollment. McCosh, by his gifts and tact, became popular away from home, and

44

Princeton, like other universities, began its career as a national institution. McCosh was a great teacher and so reasonable, intelligent, and convincing that he is to this day an example of Wilson's concept of a leader. He encouraged athletics and outdoor sports but at the same time led and participated personally in the intellectual life of the student body. With all due respect to academic administration as a profession, there is no other way except participation. McCosh surprised the world and supported orthodox religion by accepting as true the theory of biological evolution. His statement on this issue is justly famous: "When a scientific theory is brought before us, our first enquiry is not whether it is consistent with religion, but whether it is true. If it is found to be true, on the principle of the induction of Bacon, it will be found that it is consistent with religion." Here is no truckling compromise, but a manly and straightforward, as well as perspicacious, statement.

There were many changes at Princeton that anticipated the modern university. McCosh knew foreign universities, and his intention was to bring Princeton to a point where it would, without ceasing to consider its own situation and origin, rival them in effective eminence and possibly surpass them in merit. Teaching was greatly improved, and even freshmen had contacts with full professors. Juniors and seniors began specialization, a specialization not based on whim or casual preference but limited by reasonable controls. There was thus begun, with Eliot on the one side and McCosh on the other, the contest, long continued and still waged, about whether in institutions of higher education the course of study should be a matter of free election by the student or of curricular dictation. The issue is dogmatic, and I have always despised it because it justifies unwise specialization. But in the matter I side with Princeton or with Harvard according to which of them is willing to consider facts and be reasonable. Early in my Princeton career, I heard Woodrow Wilson declare, "I know better than any sophomore what that sophomore ought to study," and there is much merit in what he said. Lectures, commonly used as a means of instruction in Scotland and Germany, were introduced at Princeton sparingly at first, for the idea still prevailed that for the best results students should be met in small sections for purposes of explanation, discussion, and examination.

There was also a clear recognition of research as a university function, and under McCosh scholarships and fellowships had their practical beginning. McCosh knew, as all really great university and college presidents have known, that the strength of every such institution lies in its faculty. This truism, in the American quest for numbers, buildings, and popularity, has been often forgotten, but in McCosh's time, and long afterwards, a professorship was a free vocation; the idea that the university professor is a mere employee did not exist. Princeton grew and prospered during McCosh's administration and grew in a right way. It is my opinion that Princeton had a unity derived largely from the leadership of McCosh that has not been well understood or given its proper weight. The scholarship of McCosh, the human quality of his administration, his ability in practical affairs, even his attractive idiosyncracies are common knowledge, yet the ideology behind these attributes, which constituted the shaping force of the institution, is more elusive.

McCosh's *Laws of Discursive Thought* (1870) is certainly one of the most rational treatises on formal logic of the nineteenth century, as it is one of the simplest and least hedged in by tradition and formalism. His well-known criticism of Kant, Hegel, Hamilton, Mill, and Spencer follows the same procedure. McCosh rejected the fundamental assumption of these philosophers that the universe is, when revealed, a complete fulfillment of ideal perfection. He objected to

46

its *a priori* method and its use of the hypothesis for the supposed discovery of absolute truth in the form of fragments that might be compared to the stones, arches, beams, and girders of a perfect and perennial house of truth. He might not have denied such a concept of perfection, but he objected to a *schema* based on ratiocination and seemed unconvinced of the existence of an absolute scientific truth. His constant theme was resort to fact and observation, and his logic was strongly based on careful induction leading to exact definition. This, it will be seen, identifies him with the most modern philosophers of science. He would have admitted the necessity of infinite care in the examination of phenomena and of careful deduction, but at that point he parted company with the philosophy of the scientific method. His logic also put McCosh in opposition to Germany and its methodology, a methodology destined to conquer the world, including Princeton. I do not say that opposition to the philosophy of absolute truth was always clearly understood, but I think McCosh understood it more clearly than any other man of his time. There is no doubt that he taught, enforced, and disseminated his philosophy. If the best thought of our age may be accepted as a criterion of truth, I would suggest moreover that McCosh and his method were defeated, not on grounds of truth, but by the fashion for and preoccupation with sciences. The cause of continued and careful research, refusal to operate *a priori* according to man-made theories, and the determination of truth after complete comprehension by cognitive process were not lost, but, if we may believe the teachings of Russell, Whitehead, and other relativistic thinkers, merely deferred. McCosh's pupils went away to Germany and came back glittering with the paraphernalia of the new scientific approach. Some did not go (Wilson among them), or, if they did go, they returned, as Ormond did, unconvinced.

Wilson went to the Johns Hopkins University with high hopes; it was "the best place in America to study." There is evidence that he thought he would learn the new historical method and profit by it. He worked sincerely on suggested projects and no doubt expected to undertake the proof of a formal thesis. But the routine exercise and the formal course of study did not commend themselves to him. He began to criticize the teachings of the university as too hasty and too great in quantity. He preferred to read "much" but not on "many" subjects. He finally went to Professor H. B. Adams and "confessed" that he preferred to work on his own theme, that of American constitutional government, and Adams showed a greatness of his own by agreeing with Wilson and by offering him aid and encouragement.

I know of no evidence that Wilson was consciously hostile to the German method. I wish that he had been. It was certainly not apparent in his choice of social scientists for the faculty at Princeton. It is clear that he simply followed his bent in the search for truth, a way of working he had learned from McCosh. He no doubt respected the scientific method —as who does not?—but realized that it was not for him. Certain historical critics have found fault with Wilson as a historian largely because the work was not done according to their pattern, but it is only fair that it should be looked at in the light of the epistemology according to which it was done. Wilson sought by hard, conscientious work to arrive at what he believed to be true. This statement expresses his attitude but only suggests his philosophy.

McCosh began his logic with an essay on what he called "the Notion." By it, he meant the term in syllogistic reasoning. This may be called definition, and it may be inferred that the term must belong to the class it is said to belong to and not to another. McCosh took the greatest care in his treatment of abstraction or generalization in arriving at his

48

"notion," and it is interesting to observe that this is not characteristic of traditional Aristotelian logic but is the first principle of symbolic logic. It may be an indication that McCosh anticipated the latter. Careful correctness in generalization is moreover in line with McCosh's recognition of sound induction as the only basis of truth. It is perhaps best treated in *A Defence of Fundamental Truth,* McCosh's critique of John Stuart Mill's philosophy. It is not out of season to attribute to McCosh a full accord with the principle now widely stressed that the context of generalization must be consistent, the doctrine, that is, of the correct formation of classes, and, of course, the context of generalization should be as complete as possible. In the language of logic, one would say that the intention of generalization should be consistent and its extension, controlled by the warrant of correct observation, as great as possible. With great perspicacity McCosh saw in Mill the dangerous fragmentation that has resulted from a merely hypothetical approach to truth— dangerous because, if unchecked, it results in partial truth or half-truth, which is merely a form of error. Some of the reasoning for which McCosh indicted Mill provides perfect examples of the fallacies that have beset the scientific method when applied to other than scientific subjects.

McCosh recognized the danger in the method and fought it skillfully and vigorously, but the tide was against him, and he was pigeonholed as "a follower of the Scottish school." He had, however, many disciples in the Princeton that I entered in 1898, but none of them, so far as I know, was sufficiently conscious of the issue to debate it in McCosh's behalf. McCosh stated several times that truth varies in availability and pointed out that in certain areas probability takes the place of truth. Ormond was his best defender and did not hesitate to raise his voice against the scientific method when it was elevated into a philosophy. Wilson was truly a

follower of the methods of McCosh, but he had little interest
in methodology and logic and perhaps did not realize their
bearing on his own work. The leaders of Princeton in my
early years there were, I think, almost all of them, workers
in the McCosh tradition, and the surprising idea I should
like to suggest is that Princeton, although somewhat abashed
and defeated, was right, and Germany was wrong. This
"right" and this "wrong" need to be qualified. If the logic
and the epistemology that McCosh taught Princeton anticipated, as I think they did, the best and most recent logic and
epistemology of our own age, and if the philosophy back of
the rigorous scientific method in the process of being imported from Germany was different from this newest philosophy of our own time, as I think it was, then, solely with
an eye to the future, McCosh's Princeton was right and Germany was wrong. One must make allowance, however, for
the infinitely more important work of German scholars and
the morale that lay back of it.

I have spoken of McCosh's logic and intend to discuss his
epistemology but meanwhile wish to make a suggestion. The
philosophy of science in our learned world was, and is still,
effective in the outer rim of tangibility, a philosophy based
on empiricism and a sharp distinction between matter and
spirit (now discredited), and on the narrow use of the hypothesis as the only tool fitted for the discovery of truth. In
the fields that McCosh vaguely described as open only to
probability, the scientific method has resulted in fragmentation, departmentalization, and specialization instead of
totality and unity. This demands correction by a broader
epistemology, such as that held by McCosh and now a leading feature of the epistemology of relativistic thinkers. I am,
however, well aware that it makes not the least practical difference what I think, since, according to current learned
opinion, a professor of English literature cannot possibly

know anything beyond his subject; but there is a certain liberty in this black-out, and I can at least express the opinion that the philosophy of McCosh and his learned pupils was by no means so unproductive of truth as perhaps it was thought to be.

In describing the epistemology openly held by the greatest philosophers of science in our age, I shall not be technical. There is first the belief that science in a broad sense cannot hope to arrive at a complete and final construction of truth; in other words, that what seem to be unquestionable findings are integral parts of an ideally perfect whole. So-called scientific principles are now regarded as working bases. It was the violation of this belief (of course with a differing terminology) for which McCosh indicted Mill, and it constituted his basal objections to the doctrines of Kant, Hamilton, and Hegel. According to McCosh, idealistic speculation was not to be allowed to separate the inquiring mind from actual fact and definite event.

Secondly, the mind arrives at a perception of truth by way of the completest possible comprehension. This is a big order, but it is claimed that in the welter of process truth emerges simply and naturally, or, as Whitehead puts it, "reality is just itself." That is to say, the perception of truth is an immediate result of cognition, on the basis of complete understanding. Except for the factual truth of details and their classification, truth does not demand verification, debate, or defense. To spend one's time answering erroneous theories is to waste it, for truth does not reside in the endless jar of pro and con. To the process I called cognition McCosh and his disciples applied the word *intuition,* a subject elaborately studied in *First and Fundamental Truths* (1889) and *The Intuitions of the Mind* (1872). In earlier times it had been thought of as divine guidance. Regardless of what it is called, it is clear, strangely enough, that McCosh with all his orthodox theology did not confuse what he called intuition with revelation.

Wilson's work illustrates better than his creed the epistemology of McCosh, especially in two aspects: Wilson saw the necessity of tremendous labor in arriving at a knowledge of truth and was committed to it by his whole career; for example, by his belief that current event is future history and that all events are in causal sequence to the remotest times. He was, he said, not interested in facts but in the significance or the "meaning" of facts, and he groaned over the vast task laid upon him. Understanding of an event having been achieved, the determination of truth was strictly his affair, and he allowed no man, living or dead, to impose judgments or interpretations upon him. It may consequently be said that Wilson's specialty was being right. This statement may be followed up in detail in many fields.

Finally, there is the matter of correct procedure in abstraction, or, let us say, in the formation of classes, that was mentioned above in connection with McCosh's logic. McCosh was certainly conscious of the necessity of this correct procedure. Wilson perhaps was not, but he followed it like a bloodhound on a trail. I speak from personal experience when I say that no man could have been more impatient with what he called "sloppy thinking" than he. When you went before him with a report, it had to be clear and intelligent or you were put out of court, not always gently. Wilson demanded to know exactly what things were like, what had happened, and why. It is certainly allowable to interpret this trait as "meticulous care in the formation of classes," or, if you prefer, "abstraction based on a context of generalization pure in intention and properly limited in extension."

It is unnecessary to illustrate at great length McCosh's realistic epistemology, since illustrations are everywhere in his works; but the following passages and paraphrases from

The Scottish Philosophy may be suggestive and may add some clarity and interest to what has been said.

Bishop Butler "was convinced that, as some subjects from their nature are capable of demonstration, so others admit of only probable proof, and he had great doubts of the validity of all metaphysical arguments in behalf of the existence of Deity."

Francis Hutcheson, actuated by the various degrees of evidence adapted to various subjects, was led to treat morals as a matter of fact, and "not as founded on the abstract relation of things."

Of Hutcheson, "he everywhere appeals to facts; he brings all theories to the test of the operations of the human mind as disclosed to consciousness . . . he sets no value on speculations built up in any other way; and he everywhere speaks doubtfully or disparagingly of the logical distinctions and verbal subtleties of the schoolmen, and of the rational deductions of Descartes and Samuel Clarke."

"As to the much agitated question of the principle of individuation [Hutcheson] comes to the sound conclusion that it is to be ascribed to the nature of the thing existing."

Hamilton's "whole philosophy turns round those topics which were discussed in Kant's great work [*Critique of Pure Reason*], and he can never get out of those 'forms' in which Kant set all our ideas so methodically, or lose sight of those terrible antinomies, or contradictions of reason which Kant expounded, in order to show that the laws of pure reason can have no application to objects, and which Hegel gloried in and was employing as the ground principle of his philosophy."

"Both Hamilton and Cousins might perhaps "have had some of their views expanded, if, along with their scholarship, they had entered more into the inductive spirit of modern physical researches. But the age of universal knowledge is past, and it is vain to expect that any human capacity will contain all learning."

"The first of the volumes [of Sir William Hamilton's *Metaphysics*] is on philosophy generally and on mental philosophy in particular. He begins by recommending the study, gives the definitions, unfolds the divisions, explains the terms with amazing erudition and unsurpassed logical precision, and dwells largely on consciousness, its laws and conditions. The reading of this volume will prove as bracing to the mind as a run up a hill in the morning on a botanical or geological excursion is to the body. We especially recommend the reading of it to those whose pursuits are usually of a different character, as, for example, to those who are dissipating their minds by light literature, or whose attention has been directed exclusively to physical facts, and who have thus been cultivating one set of faculties which God has given them, to the neglect of others, and have thus been putting their mental frame out of proper shape and proportion,—as the fisher, by strengthening his chest and arms in rowing, leaves his lower extremities thin and slender."

And this from *The Intuitions of the Mind* (1882):

The mind has certainly the capacity of perception before it actually observes an external object, and the power of comparison before it can notice relations, and, in acknowledging the distinction, we must ever protest against the idea that any universal or necessary truth can be discerned by the mind without a process of *a posteriori* induction and arrangement. So far as the phrase is applied to general maxims, it should be on the understanding that they have been drawn by logical process out of the individual *a priori* convictions. ... Closely allied to the question of *a priori* is the question, Can there be an *a priori* science?[1]

And this question is the principal one now before the scholarly world. At least it is in my field of English literature.

1 P. 312.

54

Patton held this same philosophy, which, it will be seen, is efficacious in proving the existence of God and the truth of the Christian religion. We who heard Patton preach many sermons knew that, however varied the text, the sermons were logically only one—a beautifully and practically varied presentation of God's existence and the truth of religion in terms of the epistemology of the Scottish school. As for Wilson, he never lost his admiration for McCosh and never swerved from the doctrine of the obviousness of truth.

Since the obviousness of truth is a doctrine that concerns us deeply in this study, it will be investigated in some detail. Wilson was not a reader of philosophy, but, with certain casual variations, he never ceased to see in the principles of his youth, which were the philosophic atmosphere of Mc-Cosh's Princeton, the one and only road to truth. His adherence to this belief appears in many of his statements and is confirmed by his political and historical work. Consider, for example, the following paragraphs from a letter to Horace Scudder, July 10, 1886:

I want to come at the true conception of the modern democratic state by way of an accurate exposition of the history of democratic development. I want to keep safely within sober induction from concrete examples of political organization and of realized political thought. I would read the heart of political practice, letting political theory wait on that practice and carry weight only in proportion to its nearness to what has actually been accomplished. I would trace the genesis and development of modern democratic institutions—which, so far, seem to me expressions of the adult age of the State, the organic people come to its self-possessed majority and no longer in need of the guardianship of king or aristocracy or priesthood—as Maine has traced the genius and development of modern legal systems.

Just as most economists have, until very lately, deduced

their whole science from certain hypothetical states of fact and an analysis of certain fictitious kinds of men, so most writers on politics have—like Hobbes, Locke, Rousseau, *et id omne genus*—evolved government out of primitive conditions of mankind for the actual existence of which they could adduce no sort of evidence. They adopted the method common among novelists of a certain class—of creating collections of dissected qualities and then bringing about situations in which those qualities could put on the similitude of real persons: a method opposite to the dramatic, the Shakespearean method—of setting forth words and actions, and *so* letting characters emerge. As we can know persons only from what they say and do, and the manner of their acting and speaking, so we can know governments only from what *they* say and do and the manner of their speech and action. But in governments and persons alike we can look beneath the surface, if we have discernment enough, and so discover more of *character* than any amount of *a priori* speculation can reveal. . . . [My thought] is that the true philosophy of government can be extracted only from the true history of Government.

The method is unmistakable and is confirmed by Wilson's references to what he usually called "insight." Note the following passage from his review of John W. Burgess' *Political Science and Constitutional Law:*

A state cannot be born unawares, cannot spring unconsciously into being. To think otherwise is to conceive mechanically, and not in terms of life. To teach otherwise is to deaden effort, to leave no function for patriotism. If the processes of politics are unconscious and unintelligent, why then this blind mechanism may take care of itself; there is nothing for us to do. . . .

The method of political science, on the contrary, is the interpretation of life; its instrument is insight, a nice understanding of unsettled, unformulated conditions. For this lat-

56

ter method Mr. Burgess's mind seems unfit. . . . He has strong powers of reasoning, but he has no gift of insight.[2]

Wilson makes a similar criticism of Rhodes's *History of the United States,* a notable example of the scientific historical method. H. B. Fine, one of the most intelligent and reliable of witnesses, says of Wilson's adherence to large principles matured with the utmost care in his own mind: "They seemed to have for him the authority of unquestioned truths. It was apparently impossible for him to make allowance for the elements of doubt and uncertainty of the convictions of men in general."[3] This was true in the final stage, but it does not rule out long and open-minded thought. Wilson's conception of the nature of his own subject was, however, such an established belief, for he was committed to the labors and cautions necessary to the establishing of the true Baconian induction always demanded by McCosh, and his adherence to truth was a matter of honor and conscience.

To my mind the rival philosophies during the crucial epoch we are considering are matters of importance, as there was scarcely a proposal or a decision made during that time that was not in some way related to their tenets. To understand the situation, it is necessary to consider what had actually happened, and to rid ourselves of the task, it is only necessary to believe that it makes no difference what people believe. The followers of Descartes had gradually arrived at a deductive epistemology usually thought of as the scientific method and point of view. To strictly manipulable phenomena, it applied and still applies. I mean to the material part of the dichotomy of matter and spirit, a division which is no longer made. When, however, one enters mixed areas in which experiment has small or doubtful utility in estab-

[2] *Public Papers,* I, 194–95.
[3] *Life and Letters,* II, 238.

lishing truth, the scientific method is and has been unsatisfactory. In the late nineteenth and early twentieth centuries, historians and students of society began, with superior accuracy and a high degree of theoretical formalism, to carry the scientific method over into intermediate fields and even into the center of life. Those fields became narrowed and full of error and multitudinous unwarranted classifications. This state seems to exist in my own field. Such cataloguing and classifying departed from the scientific method only in its futility and its discouragement of creativity; whereas the older Baconian induction, agreeing as it did with the necessity of examining data, but differing in its perception of truth, seemed at that time, and seems at present, far better suited to the study of human life and its arts than does the scientific approach, with its fragmentary and often incorrectly generalized results. For such investigations, and even for the interpretation of the findings of science, the older method was simpler, more natural, and now predominates. It demanded the completest possible knowledge and comprehension of a subject, and incorporated the belief on that basis that the mind, by its native insight, would bring forth an answer or explanation that had the greatest chance to be true. Younger generations of scholars can hardly realize how the deductive positivity of German scholarship swept the learned world, but they may imagine the faint-heartedness of the older scholars when they reflected that they had not studied in Germany and lacked the hallmark of the new Ph.D.

Wilson had the honesty to doubt the value of the new methods when applied to history and political science, but he never worked out fully the philosophical grounds of his own position. In his later years at Princeton, he perhaps became reconciled to the German intellectual invasion, but always in practice, and intermittently in theory, he followed the method in which he had been trained. At the very time when the scientific historical method had an almost general vogue, he suspected it of collecting facts for the sake of the facts themselves and declared that "the history of nations is spiritual, not material, a thing not understood but of the heart and the imagination."[4] What he had to say about science makes his position reasonably clear:

I have no indictment against what science has done: I have only a warning to utter against the atmosphere which has stolen from laboratories into lecture rooms and into the general air of the world at large. . . . Science has not changed the nature of society, has not made history a whit easier to understand, human nature a whit easier to reform. It has won for us a great liberty in the physical world, a liberty from superstitious fear and from disease, a freedom to use nature as a familiar servant; but it has not freed us from ourselves.

It should be noted that to Wilson style was a fundamental matter, many of his expressions of opinion being presented under that caption. The word *style* is unfortunate in that it suggests rhetoric for its own sake, but it must be remembered that Wilson ties the word in with persuasion and seems to regard it as an instrument of moral and intellectual reform. His use of the word probably grew out of his feeling that truth, if it is to be itself, must be impeccably clad. From this point of view Wilson's belief in style may be regarded not only as an expression of his artistry, but as a necessary part of the total comprehension in which he believed. The agreement of Wilson's method and point of view with both an older, important school of philosophy and the latest philosophy of science may at some time justify a reappraisal of his work as a historian and social scientist. It has been pointed out that his demand was for the highest degree of proba-

4 *Ibid.,* II, 12, 35; also in *Public Papers,* I, 282–83.

bility in fundamental principles, that he pursued his search with indefatigable patience, and that he was careful that the criteria of generalization should be consistent with one another and with the final proposition. This explains why Wilson dwelled on thoroughness and why no man had a deeper zeal for order and exactitude than he; also why he relied on *insight* as an operative essential and why his universal quest was for meaning. It is to be observed that his greatest successes were in fields in which his mastery was at a high point of effectiveness. Two of his political and historical works, *Congressional Government* and *Division and Reunion,* are cases in point.

The foregoing sketch of the philosophy of James McCosh has been included to aid in understanding what the Princeton of 1898 was in origin and essence. President McCosh, moreover, applied his philosophy to education. Further, he may be ranked as a specialist in psychology. A great teacher, he had the power of convincing his students of the soundness of his own philosophy, which demanded care in the determination of truth and honesty in its acceptance. He created in his pupils profound and lasting respect for himself. These statements are not merely the result of hearsay, for when I arrived at Princeton, it still echoed with McCosh's wisdom and courage. In his inaugural address, he expressed his belief in the innate power of the individual (another modern idea), which he hoped to "draw out" or educate. It may be freely inferred that he had great faith in the potentialities of youth. He seems to have been free of that modern form of intellectual snobbery that presumes to rate human powers with mechanical exactitude as well as that that despises knowledge. He showed that he regarded knowledge as the material of truth and the means of arriving at it. It is characteristic of his democratic spirit that he knew that knowledge is power, and most interesting that in his inaugural address he protested against the academic practice of using the acquisition of knowledge as a means of discipline, his protest suggesting the concept of a free and friendly relation between educated men and the corpus of human learning. His attitude was also that of Woodrow Wilson.

As a philosopher, McCosh was probably wasted on Princeton, but not as a teacher and leader. I arrived at the university about the right time to observe his pupils and benefit from the harvest of his sowing.

McCosh had no objection to the intrusion of vocational studies into the curriculum of the university but insisted as sharply as Wilson that, when they did intrude, they must be enlightened by science and philosophy. I am aware that in this matter many educational institutions are cheating the nation, for I see, as clearly as Wilson saw, that the state has no proper interest in increasing the skills of those who will merely prey upon the people. McCosh also believed, as did Wilson, that university teachers should be leaders in research and productivity and that such scholarship is an aid and not a hindrance to effective teaching. All American universities with which I am familiar profess this faith, but I know of none that make adequate provision for its application. Apparently the American university teacher must pay for the privilege himself and be stout enough to serve his own career as scholar or scientist in addition to his teaching. The situation worried me for a long time, and I still think there are many cases of unfairness, but I now believe it may be in the fundamentals of the job. McCosh, however, made himself quite clear on the subject: "Those who are placed in the offices of a university should aim at something more than being merely the teachers of a restricted body of young men. The youths who are under them will be greatly stimulated to study by the very circumstance that their professor is a man of wide sympathies and connections with the literature or science of the country." (This explains why it was exciting and gratifying to study under Winans and Ormond.)

McCosh made liberal allowance for a *studium generale* including new subjects as well as old, but in his common-sense fashion declared that there must be a possibility of choice, for to cover the whole field in a four-year course "would give but a smattering of all without a real knowledge of any." It was he who suggested a program which became generally accepted, namely, courses in general education in the first two years and specialization in the last two. This practice, though frequently shattered by the greed and self-conceit of individual departments, is still in operation. McCosh put the theory in the long-forgotten terms of Mount Pisgah: "Let the student first be taken, as it were, to an eminence, whence he may behold the whole country, with its connected hills, vales, and streams lying below him, and then be encouraged to dive down into some special place, seen and selected from the height, that he may linger in it, and explore it minutely and thoroughly." I see nothing here about I. Q. tests or courses in vocational guidance.

I have been unable so far to find any essential differences between what McCosh sought to do in the early days, when reforms were yet small and inexpensive, and what Wilson sought to accomplish some thirty years later. However, one fact is undeniable: although both men were frankly interested in buildings and equipment, they both resorted to the only effective course that has ever built up a university—the acquisition of more and better men on the faculty. Both made a very definite effort to raise the intellectual level of the student body, using a first-rate faculty as the principal means. Wilson also made a definite effort to change and improve the social environment of the undergraduate body, for reasons that will presently become apparent. McCosh said that he wished to create at Princeton an intellectual atmosphere like that of Oxford and Cambridge and that he wanted "new chairs of literature and science." President Patton inherited McCosh's faculty, and I reached Princeton in time to know some of McCosh's first choices. It has seemed to me that he broke about even in successes and failures among them, but the group that he had brought up himself were for the most part men of high quality and constituted the strength and substance of the faculty with which I first became acquainted. It is not my purpose to name individuals in either group. The faculty I knew was a large and varied body, and my generalization is, of course, only roughly accurate. To what actual extent the education received at Princeton by faculty members had been supplemented by study in Germany, and, still more important, to what extent this study had resulted in altered attitudes, I do not know. What I want to suggest is that the leading men in the Princeton faculty of 1898 had had to some degree a common experience and had been strongly influenced by the philosophical opinions of McCosh and also by his practical ideals of performance. Some of them had studied in Germany and had brought back a new gospel, the scientific method. They felt and modestly expressed their own superiority, a superiority which was by that time recognized throughout the learned world.

I have tentatively suggested that the complete adequacy of the scientific method needs to be called in question, for there seem to be vast and important areas of human learning for which, unaided, it is not adequate. Its *a priori* approach needs, in discursive, nontangible fields, supplementation by the *a posteriori* doctrines of McCosh and Wilson. It has even been suggested that, at least as far as a philosophy of education is concerned, Princeton had at hand a better system of ideas, doomed though it was, than that which was being imported from Germany.

CHAPTER III

The Reformation

I HAVE SAID THAT at the beginning of the present century Princeton had new and difficult problems to solve. The number of students had increased, and the size of the faculty had not kept pace with the growth of the student body. The lecture method of instruction, particularly in the preceding two years, had taken the place of the traditional daily recitation, and with this development the system of the free election of courses had opened wide holes through which idle students might slip with a minimum of effort. The Princeton clientele had undergone change, and going to college had become a fashionable rather than a useful activity. A new leisure class, not without merit of its kind, had discovered Princeton as well as Harvard and Yale. The economic basis of this change was a new nationwide prosperity. Princeton had become aware of new obstacles set in the way of the cultivation of the intelligence and the salvation of the soul. These new difficulties were common and affected many institutions.

That Princeton had a conscience and that the tenderness of that conscience was a witness of the excellence of the men responsible for Princeton has been positively stated. I deprecate and despise the human habit of seeking scapegoats,

of blaming general, irremediable evils on individuals. Therefore, if anyone expects me to attack men whom I honored and
admired, such as Andrew Fleming West, John Grier Hibben,
Frances Landey Patton, and Samuel Ross Winans, all of
whom befriended me, that person must be disappointed. I
have affection and reverence for Princeton and wish it well;
in my judgment, so did its faculty during the period under
discussion. I have related that in the second semester of 1901
a discontent of which I had been unaware grew to a head,
and that the faculty ordered the appointment of a committee
to investigate university standards of scholarship, and also
that I was permitted by the simple democracy of those days
to attend the meetings at which that report was presented
and discussed.

The minutes of the Princeton faculty for March 26, April
9, 11, 14, and 16, 1903, show very general participation in
the discussion of "The Report of the University Committee
on Scholarship." At the end the minutes simply say, "It was
resolved that the Report be recommitted to the Committee."
The report is given in full. It is not well thought out and
compares rather poorly, as will be revealed, with the report
on the curriculum adopted by the faculty in April, 1904. It
is directed towards the correction of abuses, but in some
measure anticipates the later enactment. The provocative
point at issue is contained in an opening paragraph, which
asserts that scholarship at Princeton, particularly in the two
upper years, is in a state of demoralization. The plan of study
is faulty and cannot be remedied as long as instruction is
given almost entirely by lectures. A majority of juniors and
seniors make up their electives of lecture courses. The number of studies is too large, and the result is the scattering of
the students' interests and the dissipation of their energies.
Students choose their courses according to the convenience of
the hour at which a course is scheduled—all too true, one

student in my day who objected to climbing stairs even making up his schedule from courses that met on the first floor of Dickinson Hall.

Since the specific recommendations made by the committee are at least suggestive of perennial problems, they are included here: (1) The curriculum for the first three years should be such as to provide a purely collegiate type of education; (2) instruction in the freshman and sophomore years should take the form of oral recitation; (3) the freshman year should remain unchanged; (4) sophomore electives should also be recitation courses; (5) a substantial portion of the time in junior and senior courses should be devoted to oral and written tests, oral preferred; (6) upper-class courses should occupy three instead of two hours and should be five instead of seven in number for each student; (7) all junior courses should be of a general, and not a specialized, nature; (8) every junior should take one course in philosophy and one in science; (9) junior-senior courses should be abolished; (10) all four classes should be ranked on the basis of five groups; (11) General Honors should continue to be awarded; (12) as soon as funds permit, a four-course, twelve-hour schedule should be established for the best students; (13) a faculty committee should be appointed to exercise supervision over the choice of electives and the awarding of honors; and (14) the revised course of study, detailed at the end of the report, should, if possible, go into effect in the next academic year.

In fact, this report reflects the growing pains of a college developing into a university, but the thirteenth article has teeth in it and the new course of study and the attack on the lecture method of instruction are definitely corrective. It has seemed to me, however, that the prevailing excitement arose from the alarm of an essentially great faculty at what they had come to regard as the low state of Princeton education.

66

That it was actually or comparatively low I am not convinced.

The committee had worked carefully and with great sincerity. Indeed, there was about them and their report, and about the faculty who proceeded to debate the issues involved, a depth of both feeling and thought that is hard to realize. The recommendations were severe but not drastic, and I have sometimes wondered whether or not the tensity of the committee and of the overwhelming majority of the faculty who favored the report may not have been due to a modest reluctance to seem to attack colleagues who they thought were doing injury to the university. The feeling of the faculty of those days was fraternal, but the attack nevertheless proceeded. Nearly every established member of the faculty spoke, and at his best. To their minds, much was at stake, and feeling was high. New ideas and devices, some of them of the crackpot variety, were suggested. Wilson, who was a member of the committee, spoke a number of times, briefly and to the point. I shall never forget a great oration on reform by Alexander T. Ormond. The climax of the discussion I do not remember in the same terms as have been used by others who have described it. President Patton presided over the long debates, but took little or no part until the end. At the last meeting he left the chair and spoke against the adoption of the report. When his speech was ended, Wilson, who was apparently at that time in charge of the report on the floor, arose and quietly moved that the report be referred back to committee. The meeting adjourned, and the faculty departed in somewhat the same way as those who have attended a great funeral leave a cemetery.

This is ticklish ground, and I have no desire to set myself up as an authority. But I remember what Patton said and I understand the philosophy of higher education back of his speech. His principles were not secret, subtle, or shameful. They were merely those held at that time by English educators. Patton said that in our society students, scholars, bookmen, and investigators are and will remain a self-chosen group, in practice relatively small. Whatever wishful thinking and evangelical enthusiasm may urge upon us, this is true, and Patton was merely following the inherited and acquired philosophy that made him and his creed submit to fact. It is true that learning depends on the volition of the individual. I do not know of any evidence that Patton meant to kill the report, and its withdrawal has always seemed to me a doubtful act from the point of view both of parliamentary practice and of fair play. He was a famous debater and was on the floor. Why shouldn't the faculty have considered all sides of the action proposed?

Out of this issue arise two questions: Can the number of the studious be increased? Shall the non-studious be permitted to enjoy the casual benefits of university life? With reference to the second, it is perhaps enough to say that they actually do. Like the poor, they are always with us. In reply to the first question, I think the number of the studious can be increased, but in normal conditions, not in any wholesale fashion. The fundamental principle of the will to do still stands, but I agree with Wilson that a man may come to himself, even that the contact with ideas and achievements afforded by university teaching and learning may assist in bringing about the end sought. A certain zest is lent to the occupation of teaching by the fact that the adventure seems sometimes to be one of discovery in the almost unknown land of human possibilities. With more particular consideration I am disposed, in part on economic and moral grounds, to think that a student who, after a fair trial, turns out to be a loafer ought to be dismissed. Students cost a great deal more than they pay in tuition, and the funds of the state and the private foundation need to be protected. Furthermore, long and quite objective observation has convinced me that col-

The Library, Princeton University

Wilson (hat in hand) as a student with "The Alligators," his Princeton eating club, 1879.

The Library, Princeton University

Princeton faculty on the steps of Nassau Hall, 1903: J. G. Hibben (top row, far left), Wilson's successor in the presidency; (second from left), Stockton Axson, professor of English, Wilson's brother-in-law; (third row, third from left), A. T. Ormond, professor of philosophy; (third row, far right), S. R. Winans, professor of Greek and dean of the university; (third from left, second row), President Wilson; (bottom row, third from left), the author.

lege and university life, if not properly lived, has a bad influence on many students and actually robs them of the possibilities of growth and achievement that another environment might offer. But even supposing that idle students live relatively innocent lives and are, so to speak, kept out of mischief, why should colleges and universities be made into asylums for the care of young people in the dangerous years of later adolescence? The American people are certainly ignorant enough to need all the facilities provided for their education without such obvious waste. Idle students dissipate the educational energies of an institution, lower the intellectual level of the enterprise, and frequently injure themselves. There can be no objection if, in more somber mood, such students return later or seek a different environment for a new start. If they are permitted, in spite of their inefficiency, to remain in college and be graduated, they not infrequently justify the cynical statement that the worst product of a university is its alumni. These people think that they are educated, and they are not. At the risk of seeming to be old fashioned, I seriously doubt that it is "better to have come and loafed than never to have come at all." I feel the need to make my own views clear in this respect, for I wish to be fair. The problem is common and as old as the hills. The practice of putting up with shiftless students was never more widespread than it is now and, in my judgment, never gave less concern to university professors and administrators.

The two ancient English universities, Oxford and Cambridge, retained from the period of their reform in the first half of the nineteenth century a parallel system which satisfied them just before World War II. They permitted their students to be candidates either for the old pass degree system (which was carried over from the Middle Ages and which, curiously, remains the dominant feature of American higher education to this day), or for the honors system. The latter, unlike the former, implies two rather serious things: comprehensive examinations, both written and oral, and examination-room competition of a rather high order.

Candidates for a pass degree before the war took examinations periodically on parts of the syllabus, until they had satisfied all of it, thus making themselves eligible for the B. A. degree, very much as Americans do now. Honors men took the comprehensives at the end of three or four years and were ranked for degrees in the First Class, Second, Third, or Fourth. There was really no further chance in the honors system for a second try after a failure.

Some men were still attempting the pass degree at my college in Oxford, but they were not as numerous as in some of the richer foundations. Actually, there were not many of them, all told, in the entire university. As the war approached, the pass school was abolished, proving once more, I think, that the English have somewhat the best of it in this purely intellectual sphere: that it is worth while to educate only those who wish to learn; that learning, not teaching, is the basic business of higher education.

Wilson and Patton agreed with the English, but Wilson was more of an evangelist, perhaps had more faith in the possibilities of human beings. Patton was a man of brilliant intellect and noblest character. It was the fashion after his resignation to admit the former—indeed it could not be denied—and to remain silent about the latter. He did not believe in reform; why should he have said that he did? He had his own vision of a university as a place of leisurely learning having all kinds of young men within its membership, a sort of miniature well-intentioned world—no criminals, grafters, or ignoramuses admitted. I know from my own acquaintance with him that he believed in intellectual eminence and academic achievement. He took the utmost pride in the great scholars in his faculty. Wilson was the jewel of his eye. He knew the function of his great men and knew, besides, that the university existed in order that its cultural influence might be felt. He thought it was meeting with success, and so did I. Perhaps one might say, as has so often been boldly said, that Patton's conception was British and not American. He did not object to the spectacle of the young barbarians all at play, and went so far as to believe that their friendship might in future years be a source of benefit to the university. Although ordinarily this is not the case, nevertheless the natural instincts of the leisure class have often been disciplined to constructive use at Princeton.

The bill before the faculty for reforming Princeton was based on the idea of higher academic standards. I rather think Patton wished to debate it. He probably did not believe that the enforcement of high standards of performance would make students study, but the truth is that we who favored it saw no alternative. He realized that the effort to enforce these standards would be an unpleasant task and that their enforcement would send men away from Princeton for whom he thought there was a place in university life. It may be that his willingness to resign arose from his belief that such a reform should be in the hands of those who believed in it.

Certainly Patton was in agreement philosophically and morally with the men who opposed him, and in that fact there was for him both surprise and regret. The philosophy of the Scottish school had surrounded Patton and Wilson from their youth and had been for generations the reliance of Presbyterianism in both Scotland and the United States. At Princeton it had been refreshed and made vital by the teachings of James McCosh, the celebrated president of the College of New Jersey from 1868 until 1888. As I have tried to demonstrate, McCosh was a great deal more than a strong character with a Lowland Scottish accent. He was almost the last of a group of great philosophers. He taught the intensionism of Reid and defended it against Hamilton, Kant, and Hegel. This intensionism taught that there are certain constitutional principles in the operation of the human mind that determine the form of experience and, at the same time, guarantee the objective authority of its ultimate beliefs. It followed the principles of the Baconian induction and recommended special care in making these inductions complete. Intuition, or instinct, entered the operation at the point of completion, and an immediate perception of truth occurred. Wilson, Ormond, and no doubt others among McCosh's pupils followed this theory. Perhaps in the minds of other Princeton professors—Bliss Perry, for example—it was the normal procedure of unspecialized scholars in the Princeton faculty during that time. But with the influx of *a priori* method it was doomed. It is a pity that Princeton deserted the philosophy of intensionism, for its likeness to the best modern philosophy of cognition is more than merely casual. What the intensionists called intuition is by present definition an act in simple cognition that passes into the realm of higher judgments and beliefs and becomes established principle. The self-evidence arising from complete comprehension became for them, as for the relativists, the mark of accreditation. The whole operation became a necessity, and the result was the catholicity of the school.

I was away from Princeton when Wilson was elected and inaugurated president of the university, but I shared in the acclaim, approval, and wave of hope that stirred the entire Princeton community—trustees, administrators, faculty, students, and alumni. When I returned as an instructor in the autumn of 1903, Wilson was presiding over the university with a relatively increased degree of sternness. He was, moreover, very busy with rebuilding the course of study, the first major step in an extensive program of reformation. A second step had to do with the improvement of instruction, and it is possible, although I have no definite evidence, that the third was the readjustment of the social life of the student body. A fourth task, which had long been contemplated, was the building and institution of a new sort of residence college for graduate students, a project backed by Wilson.

The problem of curricular reform may be better understood after a résumé of the course of study as given in the Princeton University catalog for 1898–99. The catalog begins with a brief historical sketch of Princeton University, which makes it clear that the course of instruction continued to be based exclusively on the classical languages, leading to the degree of Bachelor of Arts, until the founding of the School of Science in 1873, when a Bachelor of Science degree was instituted, based upon "Latin, the modern languages, and the natural sciences." A department of civil engineering was added in 1875 and of electrical engineering in 1889. In the years immediately preceding 1898, postgraduate study had been systematized, mainly on paper, and the degrees of M.A., M.S., Ph.D., and D.S. were offered. The program at that point appears to be imitative of the German system. A reading knowledge of French, German, Latin, and Greek was required of all candidates for the degree of doctor of philosophy (or whom I was one). Two minor subjects in addition to the major were required for this degree; candidates took what they pleased, and the whole weight of requirement, aside from class standings, rested on a final oral examination. There was little ceremony, but my final was a tough one. On the whole, the program was a good deal like an empty form waiting to be filled.

Sixty-four professors and assistant professors and twenty-two instructors made up the faculty. Nine professors had German Ph.D.'s, and only one instructor had a doctor's degree. Princeton University gave its own tests for admission, holding examinations at Princeton and in various cities throughout the country. It is noteworthy that a very considerable body of learning was necessary to pass the entrance examinations. Today one looks with some wonder on the minimum requirements: Latin and Greek grammar and composition; Caesar, Virgil, and Cicero; Xenophon, Herodotus, and Homer; two years of French or German; and plane geometry and college alegebra. Private examination was given only with the consent of the faculty, and, without making any educational fuss about it, Princeton regularly divided its students into groups according to individual ability. It required about a quarter of a century for other universities in this country to follow suit.

Freshmen were required to take Latin, Greek, mathematics—and English, for two hours a week. The sophomore course was also mainly required: Latin, Greek, mathematics, English, French or German, plus general history (or mechanics and chemistry in the School of Science). Some choices could be made within the prescribed departments. While this curriculum was no doubt narrow, it was also useful and definite. I do not think this course of study can be blamed for defects in scholarship in the Princeton of those days. But the junior and senior years let down the bars. The junior year was completely elective except for psychology, logic, political economy, and physics, which constitute a significant exception. In the senior year only ethics and evidences of Christianity were required. There was little sequential arrangement of courses and no effective guidance. It is no wonder that with such an upper-class curriculum Princeton got into trouble. In order to clarify the program still further, I list here the electives for the junior and senior years, some of which I remember with lasting affection.

1. Moral philosophy (Patton, Shields)

2. Mental philosophy (Ormond, Baldwin, Hibben, Warren)
3. History (P. van Dyke, Frothingham, Coney, McElroy)
4. Jurisprudence and Politics (Wilson)
5. Political economy and sociology (Daniels, Wycoff)
6. Archaeology and history of art (Marquand, Frothingham)
7. Greek (H. C. Cameron, Orris, Winans, Robbins) (22 courses)
8. Latin (Packard, West, Westcott, Robinson) (26 courses)
9. Sanskrit and Avestan (Winans, Robbins)
10. English (Murray, Hunt, Perry, Covington, Tuckerman)
11. Oratory and aesthetic criticism (Perry, Covington) Included Perry's courses in poetics and prose fiction.
12. Exercises in English composition (Whig and Clio Halls)
13. German (Humphreys, Hoskins)
14. French (Harper, G. Cameron, Lewis, Vreeland)
15. Italian (Harper)
16. Spanish (Lewis)
17. Biblical literature (Patton, Hibben, Martin, Crane)
18. Mathematics (Fine, Thompson, Lovett, Wilson, Gillespie) (30 courses)
19. Astronomy (Young, Read)
20. Physics (Brackett, Magie, Loomis, McClenahan)
21. Chemistry (Cornwall, McCay, Neher, Sill)
22. Physical geography (Libbey)
23. Geology (Scott)
24. Biology (Macloskie, Scott, Rankin, McClure, Dahlgren)

Curricula of this general sort, only longer and much more heterogeneous and without the solid support of the heavy requirements of freshman and sophomore years, prevail widely in the United States at the present time. I insist that, relatively speaking, there was not much the matter at Princeton at the turn of the century.

Wilson declared in his presidential report for 1903 that the faculty was "not conveniently organized for instruction or for business" and that the curriculum was "a mere variety of studies and not a course of study." A committee of which he himself was chairman had taken up the task of "reconstruction" and was holding weekly meetings. This was regarded "as preliminary to all the plans of the University for the next generation." It was "a complex piece of business" that would require time and patience. The preliminary agreements are interesting: the freshman year was to be left substantially as it was in order that the entering students coming from a variety of schools "may be whipped into shape for the work of the years which are to follow." A "preliminary science course" to the studies of the three later years was to be introduced; this course, however, was not added. The committee planned to arrange no less than ten courses of study, which fortunately was not done, the number being reduced. This important idea was announced: "Every scientific group, for example, will be rounded by literary and philosophical studies, every literary or philosophical group by prescribed scientific courses, so that each group may be in itself, as it were, a well-considered curriculum."

He wished to draw the A.B. and B.S. courses together in a common system, and he saw that they had drawn together already. The School of Science and the Academic Department were separated by only "an artificial distinction." Students entering without Greek and having no special interest or proficiency in science pursued, as Wilson saw, discursive courses, and the distinction between them and the students registered for the A.B. was indeed artificial. To provide for these students, the committee invented a new degree, Litt. B., never popular and adopted to preserve the A.B. for those who had studied Greek. The creation of "groups" might have resulted happily in a reduction of the number of departments, but unfortunately Wilson had already reconstituted the customary divisions, appointed "heads," and formulated a set of moderate, sensible rules describing the duties of these officials. These departments were: 1. Philosophy; 2. History and Politics; 3. Art and Archeology; 4. Classics; 5. Mathematics; 6. English; 7. Modern Languages; 8. Natural Sciences; 9. Physics; 10. Chemistry; and 11. Astronomy. This action was independent of the reconstruction of the course of study then under way. It was at variance with the tendency towards combination and unification which was implicit in the reforms being contemplated by the committee. How the existence of so many departments conformed to Wilson's principles is puzzling, but it is possible that he was already listening to advisers rather than following his own ideals altogether.

The president's report for 1904 embodies the report of the faculty committee, and Wilson's own statement prepared for the board of trustees most clearly expounds the principles and ideals of the new curriculum:

The desire of all who in recent years have undertaken the reform of college studies in this country has been to form some plan by which to give consistency to the selection of studies which the undergraduate is now-a-days called upon to make among the multitude of courses and subjects of modern instruction. That is the object of our plan, and we hopefully expect it to answer its purpose. Its object is organization: to present for the use of the student an organic body of studies, conceived according to a definite and consistent system and directed towards a single comprehensive aim, namely, the discipline and development of the mind.

In order to accomplish this, and because the students who come to us and to all the larger universities of the country come with the most various and unequal preparation, it was deemed necessary to make the first, the freshman, year a year altogether of prescribed studies, and both freshman and sophomore years years devoted to subjects elementary and fundamental in character: the languages ancient and modern, mathematics, physics, logic, psychology, a modern language, and one or both of the ancient classical languages, as well as some drill in the language of his own English tongue. His addition to this of chemistry, history, and the outlines of English literature, or of a second modern language, as well as the number and thoroughness of his courses in mathematics and the languages, depends upon the election of studies he intends to make in his third year, when his attention will be concentrated upon a few subjects.

In order to direct and systematize the choice of courses in junior and senior years, the committee grouped departments under major divisions: I. under the Division of Philosophy, the Department of Philosophy and the Department of History, Politics, and Economics; II. under the Division of Art and Archeology, a single Department of Art and Archeology; III. under the Division of Language and Literature, the Departments of Classics, English, and Modern Languages; IV. under the Division of Mathematics and Science, the Departments of Mathematics, Physics, Chemistry, Geology, and Biology, Astronomy being included in this division but not erected into a separate department. It will be noticed that Wilson had the insight to associate his own department with philosophy, and it is possible that, if left to himself, he might have seen that all discursive subjects, as distinguished from the sciences, belong with it; also that the problem of mathematics remained unsolved. It forms a nexus between the two groups and should somehow have appeared in both, since other subjects besides the natural sciences have quantitative and proportional aspects.

For the accomplishment of its original purposes the arrangement was extremely ingenious, since it provided at once for sequence and co-ordination, breadth and control. In each department there were two required courses of fundamental character for those who chose the subject. In the senior year three courses, of much more intensive quality, were provided in the major field. Recently, I have been given to understand, a four-course plan has been developed, highly spoken of and thought to be an improvement. In 1904, however, the junior was required to take a second course in the division to which his major subject belonged. That left him one free elective, and it was ingeniously provided that, if he made use of that freedom of choice in his junior year along with the elective freedom of his senior year, "he may easily qualify himself for either two cognate, or even contrasted, departments in his senior year."

It is absurd to think, as is often done, that any subject stands alone and that it is not possible to make an orderly arrangement of the field of learning as regards sequence, interrelation, co-ordination, and ultimate function. The Princeton report was possibly the best attempt to that date to set the *studium generale* in order, but at least two things should be kept in mind. First, the faculty were too narrowly trained to operate in large groups, and any formulation except the departmental one went against their accustomed forms of thought; and second, no administrative officials can operate effectively in American universities unless they have control of appointments, promotions, and salaries—otherwise, their activities are mainly matters of politeness and friendly association.

The report was frankly based on the premise that "the undergraduate student is not likely to make a systematic choice of studies unless aided by more mature judgments than his own, and upon the assumption that the knowledge of men more mature than himself is a safer guide to a consistent and serviceable choice than his own untested tastes and preferences." The plan prescribed "a sort of intelligence and consistency" in a system of "assisted election." This was Princeton's polite, reasonable, and effective way of escaping from the educational and administrative evils of the free-elective system, while at the same time it sought to retain the benefits and advantages of freedom and self-direction. The need for proper guidance for students in the choice of courses has been widely felt in American universities, and much time and effort have been expended on systems of advisers. These advisers have no doubt done much good, but they have usually been armed only with moral suasion and have often lacked adequate experience and knowledge in a difficult task, so that up to now only curricular requirements have been of very great value. This report, however, at least in so far as it reflects Wilson's beliefs and opinions, is unsurpassed in my experience in its grasp of both fundamental principles and fundamental issues. Wilson says:

Some features stand out as the very essence of the plan. Its fundamental principle is, that the object of undergraduate education is general training rather than specialized skill, a familiarity with principles rather than the acquisition, imperfect at best, of a mass of miscellaneous information,— that the acquisition of information is, indeed, not education at all; that education is a training necessary in advance of information, a process of putting the mind in condition to assimilate information and know what to do with it when it is acquired: that ideas, principles, schemes of thought, and methods of investigation govern facts and determine their place and value.

About the principles expressed in this paragraph and those following it, American educators have never made up their minds; in other words, they have not decided whether universities, as distinguished, let us say, from institutes of technology, should expend their energies in teaching the techniques of trades and vocations. The current opinion seems to be that they should, but I am not sure that this thought will continue to prevail. Wilson excluded applied science from his plan and justified the exclusion in very thoughtful words:

In technical schools, moreover, no less than in the colleges, it is becoming evident, not to men of science only, but also to men who speak from a direct practical knowledge of industrial undertakings, that much more than mere skill in practical processes, learned by precept and example in the laboratories and workshops of the training schools, is necessary for the equipment of the men who are to take charge of the mechanical and chemical processes of our present industrial world. New processes must be found and used at every turn of the rapid movement of modern industry, and nothing but a very clear-cut and definite mastery of the principles of science, and of the more recondite principles at that, will supply them. Even old and familiar processes will go astray or stand unimproved in an age of improvement unless the men of skill be also men of broad theoretical knowledge in the sciences from which every process springs. Practical science gets all its sap and vitality from pure science; and the business of the colleges is plain. There is little enough time as it is in the four years of undergraduate study to teach the pure science that is fundamental: there is none in which to teach a few processes picked up from the mass and inadequately supported by theory.

. . . Some men, for lack of time or of means, must hurry into their professional work without this general orientation in the general field of study; even the so-called 'learned professions' must no doubt be crowded with men who are mere experts in a technical business, with no scientific knowledge of the principles they handle, and no power, consequently, to lift their work to the levels of progress and origination; but some, fortunately, may approach their life tasks more slowly, by a more thorough way of preparation, and it is in the interest of society that these should be as many as possible. It is our deliberate purpose to minister to these men and not to those who skimp and hurry and go half trained into their professions. And not to these only but also to those who seek or may be induced to take the general training of character which is to be had by means of the contacts and comradeships of a vital college life, the general training of mind and perfection of quality to be had from studies whose outlook is upon the broad field of all that the world thinks and does.

Bacon himself never grasped a practical issue more firmly or expressed it more clearly.

It is almost pathetic to observe in universities the perennial hope for reformation or improvement by means of curricular revision. I have been present at many such attempts, and they have always been to some extent failures and disappointments. There must be some reason why learned men should repeatedly make this attempt. Failures have been attributed, often correctly enough, to selfish political combinations within the faculty in the service of the greed or to the exaggerated, stubborn enthusiasm on the part of individuals and departments for the spread of certain subjects. Many teachers of commerce, journalism, geology, and sociology, for example, have become so convinced of the importance and extent of their subjects that they admit no propaedeutics and think that a four-year course is all too short for any substantial accomplishment. The subject in question must be begun in the freshman year and continued and increased in quantity throughout the entire course. This distortion of curriculum is seemingly recurrent and probably incurable, but there is more to it than greed, self-conceit, and political skill. The point is that the problem has not been solved because it has been approached in a wrong way. Wilson's philosophy of education represents the beginning of a more enlightened attack.

The difficulty lies in widespread ignorance of the general field of human learning and of the general philosophy of that field. A high degree of often excellent specialization has robbed the teaching profession of total comprehension and caused its members to think that the philosophy of education is itself a specialty and therefore does not concern them. The matter is very simple, so simple perhaps that it has been overlooked. A parallel to the situation might be drawn with degrees of tangibility in the field of investigation. If we think of the area of investigation as a globe, the surface of which represents the natural sciences, experiment is relatively unimpeded. Bacon's figure which compares the binding of Proteus to the forcing of matter to change and transform itself is an apt illustration of the use of scientific skill to control nature. Experiment not only can be made but can be tested by repetition. If one imagines passing from the surface to the center of this globe, tangibility, and therefore the possibility of successful experiment, decreases rapidly and in varying degrees. At the center, we may suppose, is the region of human reason, feeling, and will, of immense importance and controlling power. Here experiment is always difficult and often impossible. We may carry this illustration a little farther by placing the social sciences and the humanities at the middle distance between surface and center. Here there is some approach through statistics and casual experiment, but in general the social sciences are too discursive to be handled successfully by experimentation. We are not helpless, however; there is another method of approach.

The scientific method, as we have seen, took over at

Princeton and at other American universities at the end of the nineteenth and the beginning of the twentieth centuries, and the result is that, although the material world has been wrought upon to the profit of humanity to a degree never before equaled, the vast discursive area in which we live and move and have our being has made little true progress, indeed has been narrowed, hindered, and vitiated by an ineffectual method of attack. In simple language, these discursive fields are the area of wisdom and the conduct of life, and the investigation of these fields has to be inductive in procedure. In a preceding chapter this method has been described in McCosh's terminology as a procedure *a posteriori,* whereas the scientific method, which impinged upon his philosophy, is a procedure *a priori* or deductive procedure. Of course this antithesis is only roughly true, and both procedures are required of the thinker. The inductive method demands complete knowledge leading to a comprehensive view and relies for its comprehension on an immediate perception of truth. On the other hand, the scientific method that all but drove it out of academic investigation proceeds deductively by means of hypothetical speculation, the examination of pertinent data, and the process of verification. The conclusion is deductively arrived at as the manifestation of an inclusive theory. The point of this discussion is that history, literature, the social sciences, and philosophy itself yield their secrets to an inductive approach, not a deductive one, and, if curriculum-makers had allowed for this fact, they might have made greater and more important progress. These discursive subjects demand breadth, a larger unity, and an awareness of interrelations, and are split into impotent fragments by the application of the deductive method. Had Wilson trusted and insisted upon the rightness of his own correct method and of his inner belief, he might have accomplished even more than he did.

84

Wilson speaking at the dedication of Hamilton Hall.

The Library, Princeton University

Four distinguished Princetonians: Presidents Francis Landey Patton (upper left) and James McCosh (upper right), Dean Andrew F. West (lower left) and Professor A. T. Ormond (lower right).

The results of the application of the scientific method to discursive subjects have been the discovery of much useful information and the ordering of certain minor areas, but they have also included disregard for, or misunderstanding of, aspects of the life of the mind; and what is almost worse, the splitting of the areas studied into fragments, the manufacturing of a number of ill-based classifications, and the particularization of the whole field of learned culture, so that it reminds one of the little pens in a stockyard. We call this specialization, and it is a constant menace to truth, because it distorts in practice the comprehensive order that manifests truth. In my field, for example, there is not only an English department but as many isolated units as there are divisions of the whole area. Men teaching Anglo-Saxon or Shakespeare are as separate from their colleagues as if they were giving instruction in Semitic archeology. If this division goes on, we may expect not only a separate department of criticism but separate departments of T. S. Eliot and James Joyce. It is not enough to say that the process is unnecessary and troublesome. It is also a hindrance to rational development and to creative scholarship and authorship. A curriculum committee might not be able to change the prevailing superficiality and dissipation of thought in discursive subjects, but it would be better able to carry on if it understood them.

The case rests so far only on an illustration, but it can be supported by consideration of the best epistemology and logic of the current world. It is obvious that the scientific method is sound in the field of manipulable phenomena. The success of applied sciences shows this to be true, but the investigation of other fields by this method, however well satisfied certain workers in those fields may be, is smitten with useless divisions and permeated with the partial truth that is often but a form of error. Isolated facts are discovered and theories invented to account for them, and we have wheels within wheels. Beyond a certain point the scientific use of cause and effect simply cannot be made to apply in non-experimental fields. Induction leading, if possible, to total comprehension is both natural and necessary, and the study of the human reaction is not without hope of advancement. The theory of cognition seems to show that intellectual response is a constructive thing that may sweep through the mind in an impulse of both truth and creativity. The way now blocked with formal and theoretically erected barriers needs to be opened.

One is not therefore surprised to find that in his first view Wilson favored groups and not departments, discursive study and not formal restriction, self-directed intelligence and not so many credits. This is agreeable to me, and had I the responsibility, I should greatly reduce by combination the number of departments in the humanities and the social sciences. I should have more comprehensive examinations on subjects instead of courses and have them read by impartial examiners, and should discourage qualifying for degrees by piling up a hundred academic idiosyncracies, and I should not cut the dog's tail off an inch at a time. The fragmentation comes in part, at least, from American reliance on teaching instead of learning.

It is encouraging to know that the Princeton plan, although somewhat formalized and departmentalized in its final form, worked well. That which is true, sensible, and useful seems after all to be practical in curricular affairs. The only curriculum in my experience that rivaled it was the one in operation at the University of Minnesota in 1910— no doubt long since abandoned. It provided, as I remember, two years of a laboratory science, two years of foreign language, a certain amount of mathematics, freshman English, and two years of social science beginning with an invaluable course in history that taught the handling of documents. It provided a body of sound modern knowledge of fundamental subjects on which upper-class teachers could rely and build. Back of Wilson's curriculum was the idea that certain kinds of knowledge and training, as represented by certain departments, are of a more fundamental character than others and are therefore propaedeutic to other subjects that rest on them for principles, materials, or both. The latter should consequently be pursued later in the course of study than the selected fundamental subjects. I do not suppose that this principle has often been openly denied, but, for reasons cited above, it has in many great American universities become a dead letter. Wilson believed that it was the duty of the university to provide all of its graduates with broad training in pure sciences and the rudiments of general academic culture. This responsibility has been disregarded in many institutions and might have been lost sight of altogether had it not been for the efforts of members of the Society of Engineering Teachers and other men in purely technical fields. The present offenders are not the teachers of applied sciences but the teachers of new practical subjects in discursive areas, such as journalism, dramatics, commerce, and sociology. Although my interest is in the exposition of Wilson's opinions, I must remark that I cannot see how curriculum-makers can fail to consider the question of the sequence of courses.

However the sciences may settle this question, which seems to concern them immediately, the need is for breadth and not for specialization. This was the philosophy of learning that Wilson adhered to always. It is quite evidently the cumulative result of his earlier ideas about the course of study. Unfortunately, both as a student and as an administrator, he made concessions to the formal organization of universities, but I think that he was nevertheless ahead of his time, since the fundamentals of the educational philosophy in which he was trained have again received the support of the leading thinkers of our world. I repeat that the principle of the inductive pursuit of truth applies most directly to subjects dealing with man and society rather than to science, but scientists, too, must somehow learn the significance of what they are doing. It will be seen that Wilson's curriculum makes an effort to break down in university training the barrier between science and the liberal arts. He regarded pure science as a proper part of a liberal education. This has always appealed to me as a student of the Renaissance.

The Renaissance, not Bacon only, took all knowledge as its province, and the division, for example, between literature and science is strictly post-Cartesian. I do not know whether this separation has been beneficial to science, but I think it has been devastating to literature. With the idea of doing the best I could in the circumstances, I have steadily advised students of literature to apply themselves also to science. The foolish reply I have often received is that the area of science has grown too extensive to be casually mastered. As regards details, this may be true; but as regards principles, point of view, and main stages of development, precisely the opposite is the case. A main object of modern science has been simplification, so that the student with an ordinary textbook of physics may with reasonable application learn what physics is about from Archimedes to Einstein. Silly people forget how much time and effort in earlier days went into the learning of now discarded theory, untruth, and mere superstition.

A few more citations from Wilson's report will serve to close this account:

The baccalaureate is again made to stand for a definite, ascertainable body of training. It seems to be a practicable way of getting something like the old definiteness and discipline out of the modern multitude of studies,—for each man a definite body of training, though not the same for all.

In view of what the schools were willing and able to give us; . . . we have sought to reduce the entrance requirements to a very simple list.

And because we have made all our courses in science courses in pure science, we have put them in the same category with literary, philosophical, and general humanistic studies as a means of liberal training.

This careful study beforehand of matters like this is not a mere dictate of convenience; it affords invaluable assistance in working out purposes which are not material but of the spirit of all our hope and endeavour. This is the concrete way to express our plans for the intellectual, social, and moral life of the University, and to set our thoughts upon definite objects.

The commitee report came before the faculty in finished form, and although there was some debate, in part acrimonious, the report went through practically unchanged. At several places in the document and in earlier statements by Wilson, there is evidence that a second step in the reorganization of Princeton was contemplated; namely, measures for the improvement of teaching along with the deeper purpose of "raising the intellectual level of the student body." It is now obvious that this second step was an attempt to get the student to take his own education in hand, and, to use a familiar phrase of Wilson's, to make him come to himself.

CHAPTER IV

Humanism

Wᴵʟꜱᴏɴ'ꜱ ᴘʟᴀɴꜱ for the reformation and improvement of teaching were from the beginning matters of common, although rather vague, knowledge and of general discussion. When the change came, we were all to some extent engaged, not in the invention, but in the institution of the preceptorial system. The president had apparently thought the system out with great care and made it known to those trustees and alumni who were his friends and counselors. Money was always needed in the Wilson administration, and it seems probable that the whole enterprise was established and supported by the generosity of certain wealthy Princetonians who liked the idea and believed in Wilson. They wished Princeton to profit by his leadership. The funds were quickly provided, and the preceptorial system was set up with amazing promptitude. Practically the whole thing was done in the spring of 1905.

Wilson talked with me a number of times about the project, and I was present when he talked to groups and to the English Department about it. He was, as usual, open in mind, but it was easy to see that his original ideas had undergone some modification through the advice of the faculty by the time the preceptorial system was put into actual operation. In retrospect, I think that every change was for the worse, or rather, I should say, I believe that his rejected original ideas would have introduced into American university education certain valuable reforms. The Wilson that I knew was a most considerate and reasonable man, and I sometimes wonder if the world, the nation, and the university did not lose substantially in the modification, often no doubt with his consent, of his original ideas. That this conjecture is not mere adulation should be apparent from my explanation, in philosophical terms, of what I believe to be the basis of his genius for the determination of truth.

For example, Wilson did not think of the men to be introduced into the faculty as merely additional professors, associate professors, and assistant professors, but as a new kind of university teacher with a different object and function. The rather odd and to this day not well-liked designation of "preceptor" indicated that these men would not belong to an established academic rank. Wilson told me the title had been suggested to him by certain tutors of law students in the Inns of Court whose duties were solely advisory and instructional and who were called preceptors. He added that preceptorial duties were to him the most pleasant and important of all teaching activities. Such men, he said, might look forward to increases in salary and to all honors within the gift of Princeton and the university world.

This attitude met with powerful though gentle opposition from the start. Professors preferred to regard preceptors as subordinates and assistants and did not take kindly to the idea of having a large number of academic equals suddenly thrust into their midst. Their objection assumed a subtle form, indeed the form of a good and generous idea. "We are all preceptors," they said, and most of them did take over a share of preceptees and did excellent work, and thus got acquainted with their students. Since they were human beings, why shouldn't they do so? Wilson accepted their idea and later showed pride in it.

A stranger objection came from the preceptors themselves. They had been discontented with the formalities of university teaching, and Princeton offered them a new freedom which they thought they longed for. Some of them no doubt did desire a more vital teaching system than that which prevailed throughout the universities of the land, but they wanted to belong to the academic profession and to be labeled intelligibly. Therefore, they actually welcomed the announcement that, although locally called preceptors, they were really assistant professors in disguise. What a blessing it would have been if a great American university like Princeton had rid itself of the onus of rank among its professors, which is a useless regimentation and the breeder of jealous competition, intradepartmental politics, and often a selfish disregard for the interests of the university and the cause of learning. In any case, it is regrettable that Wilson's original plan was not carried out.

Another great modification of Wilson's plan for the independence of the preceptor was the involvement of the preceptor in the giving of examinations and the allotment of grades. This was certainly at variance with Wilson's original intention, but the issue was not directly faced. The professors felt that they were divinely selected and directed to award grades to *their* students. Grades had to be awarded. Preceptors, on the other hand, felt that they could not allow themselves to be dominated by the professors and their preceptees perhaps subjected to whim or prejudice. Therefore, the preceptors demanded a voice in the determination of grades and secured it.

There was possibly nothing else they could do, but the obvious solution, the institution of external examiners, was ignored, presumably because Princeton could not afford it or did not want it. The Oxford system was far more congenial with Wilson's idea than any system could be in which the same men direct the study and pass upon the results. The system of outside examiners puts the tutor and his pupils on the same side of the fence and makes them friends and fellow workers. Our system makes them antagonists and, furthermore, robs us of any practical way of determining the actual value of any university teacher. In general, American university teachers rate themselves as experts; it is polite to believe them, and there is no definite way of discovering the truth. Therefore the choice of teachers in our universities is often by hearsay, estimate of "personality," and departmental politics.

There were thus at least two matters in which the establishment of the preceptorial system failed to afford a model of great reform for American university education, but the sun has not set, and I recommend to Princeton and other universities a profound and sympathetic study of Woodrow Wilson's ideas about university education, for I think such a study might still yield by direct suggestion and implication many principles of great value and importance to the conduct, policy, and purpose of American higher education. In our age of diffusion of interest, quest of pleasure, and the softening of human fiber that comes from wealth and idleness, the work is all to do, and universities can unquestionably aid the strengthening of the mind and spirit against mighty forces of destruction.

However that may be, the preceptorial system was a great success, and I think it is not too much to say, since it was widely known and attracted much distinguished attention, that it had great influence in many places throughout the country. Wilson was not yet a political figure, and people did not as yet feel that any moral courage was necessary to differ with him. It was a humane and natural system and

commended itself to teachers and other citizens by its con-
tention that teachers and students should be friends and
collaborators in a worthy enterprise. In some cases it may
have reminded German-trained professors that they too were
human. The success of the system was no doubt due in part
to the ability and earnestness of the men who worked in it.
Not only did it vividly and convincingly emphasize the need
of friendly relations between students and teachers and stimulate co-operation between these groups, but it also harmon-
ized and unified their educational efforts. The organization
and operation of the system are described in Wilson's annual
report of 1905 to the trustees, which follows. His article in
the *Independent* of August 3, 1905, and his address before
the Western Association of Princeton Clubs at Cleveland
on May 19, 1906, furnish additional explanation.

After listing in his report the names of forty-seven newly
appointed preceptors with a brief academic biography of
each, Wilson continues:

These appointments followed very fortunately upon our
recent thorough reconstitution of the course of study. In
that reconsideration of the subject matter of our teaching
we gave new co-ordination to the studies of the University
and effected an arrangement which has given to the undergraduate's choice of studies a new touch of system and consistency. These changes have afforded us a definite and satis-
factory basis for reconsidering also and improving our
methods of instruction. A year ago, when I submitted my
report to you, I did not venture even to hope that I was so
soon to be able to set about reforms which for more than
twelve years past have seemed to me the only effectual means
of making university instruction the helpful and efficient
thing it should be. I have now the great happiness of realizing
that these reforms have already been effected with ease and
enthusiasm, that Princeton is likely to be privileged to show

how, even in a great University, the close and intimate contact of pupil and teacher may even in the midst of the modern variety of studies, be restored and maintained. Our object in so largely recruiting our Faculty has been to take our instruction as much as possible out of the formal classrooms and get it into the lives of the undergraduates, depending less on lectures and written tests and more on personal conference and intimate counsel. Our preceptors, with a very few exceptions, devote themselves exclusively to private conference with the men under their charge upon the reading they are expected to do in their several courses. The new appointments have not been made in the laboratory departments, where direct personal contact between teacher and pupil has long been a matter-of-course method of instruction, but in what may be called the "reading" departments. We are trying to get away from the idea, born of the old idea of lectures and quizzes, that a course in any subject consists of a particular teacher's lectures or the conning of a particular text-book, and to act upon the very different idea that a course is a subject of study to be got up by as thorough and extensive reading as possible outside the classroom; that the class-room is merely a place of test and review, and that lectures, no matter how authoritative the lecturer, are no more than a means of directing, broadening, illuminating, or supplementing the student's reading.

Accordingly, the function of the preceptor is that of guide, philosopher, and friend. In each department of study each undergraduate who chooses the department, or is pursuing all the courses offered in it in his year, is assigned to a Preceptor, to whom he reports and with whom he confers upon all of his reading in those courses. We try to limit the number of men assigned to one Preceptor so that they may not be too numerous to receive individual attention. He meets them at frequent intervals, singly or in small groups, usually in his own private study or in some ones of the smaller and quieter rooms of the University, and uses any method that seems to him most suitable to the individuals he is dealing with in endeavouring to give their work thoroughness and breadth; and the work they do with him is not of the character of mere preparation for examinations or mere drill in the rudiments of the subject, but is based upon books chosen as carefully as possible for the purpose of enabling them to cover their subjects intelligently. . . .

One way of stating the nature of the change is to say that now it is the real work of the University and not intermittent study for examinations: that the term work, as we have been accustomed to call it, stands out as the whole duty of the student; and the amount of work done by the undergraduates has increased amazingly. But this is a much too formal way of stating the change. It looks at its surface and not within it. It is not the amount of work done that pleases us so much as its character and the willingness and zest with which it is undertaken. The greater subjects of study pursued at a University, those which constitute the elements of a well-considered course of undergraduate training, are of course intrinsically interesting; but the trouble has been that the undergraduate did not find it out. They did tasks, they did not pursue interests. Our pleasure in observing the change which has come about by reason of our new methods of instruction comes from seeing the manifest increase of willingness and interest with which the undergraduates now pursue their studies. The new system has been in operation little more than two months and yet it has affected the habits of the University almost as much as if it were an ancient institution. The undergraduates have welcomed it most cordially and have fallen into it with singular ease and comprehension, and we feel that both authority and opinion are working together towards a common end,—the rejuvenation of study.

This was Princeton, not paradise, and Wilson's enthusiasm does not cause him to stray from fact. The following paragraphs from his report of 1906 add further detail and criticism:

Our new method of instruction has now had a full year's test, and has stood the test most satisfactorily. It has produced more and better work; it has systematized and vitalized study; it has begun to make reading men; and has brought teachers and pupils into intimate relations of mutual interest and confidence. I speak of it as a "system" of instruction, but we have not given it the symmetry of uniform rules of a system. We have sought to preserve the utmost elasticity in its use, in order that the individual gifts and personal characteristics of the Preceptors might have free play. Not only must instruction in each subject have its own methods and points of view, but each instructor must be as free as possible to adapt himself to his pupils as well as to his subject. What is true of all teaching is particularly true of this intimate way of associating teacher and pupil: the method is no more effective than the man who uses it. His whole makeup conditions his success and determines his character. The almost uniform success of last year's work means that the teachers were singularly fitted for the new and delicate task for which they had been selected.

There were marked varieties of success, of course. The new way of teaching demands for its ideal success a very intimate and cordial sympathy between the preceptor and his pupils, and of course not all of the preceptors have been of the temperament to make close friends of the men they taught. Some are a little too much inclined to be faithful taskmasters, the supervisors of their men's work, and the intimacy between them and their pupils is hardly more than the intimacy that must in any case come from such relations of mutual responsibility. Some have succeeded because they stimulate their men; some because they understood and helped them; some because they knew how to hold them to strict and frequent reckonings; some because they interested; others because they had the gift for congenial conference. But amidst all the variety there has been no failure, and the beginning of the second year of the system already shows interesting results in the new attitude of the undergraduates and the manifest fruits of the year of training. Each class shows a distinct stage of advance. It is not merely a year further along in the subject of study, but also a year further along in the ability to study, and in intelligence of approach and facility in work.

I accept in general, as Wilson did, the idea that learning is fundamental and is the main reliance in education and educational systems, and I therefore think the British basal idea superior to the American. That the emphasis on teaching instead of learning is powerful and prevalent in America is indicated by the initial concept of a great foundation, recently formed. Although its policy has subsequently been changed and broadened, it originally excluded scholars, teachers, and institutions of higher learning from the unrestricted use of its funds. These funds were to be devoted to the improvement of teaching and educational administration in the direction, and by the means, the foundation thought necessary. Thus the original policy did not support the individual initiative essential to learning but placed preponderant faith and emphasis on teaching as a means of social betterment.

While teaching is certainly not useless, the American habit of relying on it to the exclusion of other methods of learning is hardly justifiable. Our educational practice is not aggregative, and I think it ought to be. When some useful discovery in the field of educational method is made, we, instead of adding and relating it to the knowledge and skill we already possess, feel obliged to throw away all that tradition and experience have taught us and proceed empirically to adopt exclusively the new discovery. The mental habits we have formed, or that have been formed for us, cause us to believe that every problem or difficulty is likely to be resolved by a discovery. The new thing is presumably it. I need not say that the world of the mind as known to superior thinkers does not include this presumption.

The American mental attitude just described is easily explainable in terms of the *a priori* philosophy that has had us by the throat for a hundred years and that has recently tightened its hold by means of pragmatism. We need to realize that many problems, especially those arising in the fields of the humanities and the social sciences, including education, yield to wisdom, often slowly acquired, and not to hypotheses and hunches supported, if supported at all, by statistics and inevitably limited experimentation.

Teaching is an ancient occupation tried and tested time out of mind by the human race in nurseries, families, communities, shops, schools, and pulpits. It appears widely in the lives of lower animals as a factor in survival and evolution. It is absurd to deny its utility, but hardly less so to make of it a complete reliance and ignore the other side of the operation, which is learning. In the nature of things, teaching is futile unless the taught learn. It is also obvious that almost every touch of distinction or excellence in every field of action results from the self-propelled activity of the learner. Routine learning or mere imitation may save a creature's life, but can result in nothing beyond the commonplace. Schools and colleges have in general occupied themselves with the superior or fortunate classes of society and have sought some degree of excellence. The fact that study and effort to learn are necessary to this excellence may be the reason, along with disregard of the herd, that the English put their faith in learning, or the effort of the student; and also the reason Americans with their love of commonplace uniformity put their reliance on teaching. It may be that expert teaching by the use of routine can produce a sort of foolproof mediocrity in schools, colleges, and universities, but why not have both teaching and learning?

It was the nexus between teaching and learning, a sort of co-operation in the process of education, at which the Princeton preceptorial system was aimed, and this direction we owed to the thought of Woodrow Wilson. His faculty thought poorly of lectures and quizzes, because, operating too exclusively on the side of teaching, they did not yield full profit to the students. One could not say that under the older lecture system the gifted and the industrious did not fare as well as they could have under any other system, since they were already self-directed learners. They heard the lectures, read the books, thought about them, and galloped through the tests. The preceptorial system, it must be confessed, was of necessity aimed a little lower. Presupposing good minds and proper preparation in the secondary schools, it had, as I see it, two main objectives: first, to develop the student's understanding by asking the right questions, removing difficulties and obscurities, and introducing new tools and showing how to use them; and, second, to increase the student's interest in study so that he might go ahead on his own initiative.

The latter objective in my judgment will always be extremely difficult to bring about. Most students want to go through college worthily and avoid the disgrace of being thrown out. They are usually willing to do what is called for in the bargain, but no more. They challenge the professor or preceptor to "interest me if you can." This makes a good game, and I have played it with zest for fifty years. If students sleep in my classes, I never resort to physical means to awaken them. If I cannot do it by intellectual skill, I let them sleep. This game is worth playing. In the preceptorial groups, those who were moving under their own steam were a pure delight, and the numbers were relatively large; those who were not were polite, compliant, and not interested. This made the problem fairly clear.

Mankind is infinitely varied, and modern young men seem especially so. Wisdom, on the other hand, seems always in short supply, so that it is impractical to lay down sets of rules for the relationship between adviser and advisee, and those who do so usually betray the narrowness of their own concept of the job. One man relies on serving tea, another on a bluff and hearty manner that is supposed to indicate that he is one of the boys, while still another displays Italian prints, fine books, and curious bric-a-brac. An idea that always amused me was that Princeton students would be glad to meet and learn to know me because I was a university professor. Students often possessed great wealth and high social standing, and, if they had been rude enough to think of such a thing, they would have been obliged to feel that they, not I, constituted the condescending party. My suggestion is that we preceptors attend to business, which arises out of the issue between civilization and savagery, truth and error, skill and awkwardness, right and wrong. Let us draw up our lines on this battlefield and fight the action there. Let us use books and ideas, and let us be courageous and alive. Our side is badly in need of troops; let us recruit them. Our enemies are richer and far better organized than we.

Wilson believed in discipline and relied on comradeship in the great reformation of Princeton, and he thought that co-operation between teacher and student was the best hope of success. This idea, supported by others, is the one most fully tested in the preceptorial system. Wilson saw, as the quotation from his report of 1906 shows, that some preceptors were more successful than others and that success in getting students to study did not depend upon a single method. He claimed success for all. He did not admit, as he might have done, that some preceptors bored their preceptees and wasted their time. Some stimulated their men; some understood and helped them; some held them to strict and frequent reckonings; some interested them; some had a gift for "congenial conference." I rated myself somewhere about the median in degree of success.

I may say in partial extenuation that I was busy in Whig Hall and with my own scholarly efforts, which included the sizable task of learning the literature of our language from *Beowulf* to Mark Twain. I knew a good deal about it already, but there were great gaps to be filled in. It had moreover to be learned both accurately and discursively, for it was obvious to me from the beginning that the instant the preceptee lost confidence in the preceptor, his attention wavered and his interest slackened. That five years of broad and yet particularized study, what Whitehead calls the "habit of thoughtful elucidation," was painful but invaluable to me. In my own field I have never been at a loss since. May I therefore add to Wilson's enumeration of bases of success mastery of one's subject, a mastery so thorough that it knows regions of doubt as well as regions of certainty?

Wilson uses two words which still remain mysterious. Some preceptors, he says, "stimulated" and some "interested" their men. How does one do these things, even if one has "the gift of congenial conference"? Methods which have been used, and which I have in part enumerated, indicate wide variety. My own method, by way of illustration, is simple, for I know my stock in trade pretty well by this time, having had thousands of pupils. I am very short on tricks and devices. I plan every exercise in what seems to me a logical and common-sense way and rarely, if ever, seek effects. My professorial irony is of average quality. I distrust imported and extraneous methods as such and have, besides, this handicap—I think literature, like life itself, has to be experienced in order to be understood and appreciated. Obviously that operation is strictly the student's affair, and I can do nothing about it. I think that literature, for instance Shakespeare, teaches its own method and is, like life itself, both method and corpus. There is therefore very little to be learned from me.

I should like, however, to add one more device which I never neglect in securing the interest of my students in the subjects I teach. That is to reckon with the philosophy of learning that lies buried and unknown within them, but potent in their minds. American students have been saturated from infancy with the outworn and outmoded *a priori* philosophy of our country. If the teacher can convince them that the learning he wishes to inspire will not take up the space in their minds that they want to use for something else that they would like "to put into it," they will ordinarily consent to listen. As a whole, they conceive of their minds as literally made up of a set of pigeonholes, limited in extent; one thing in, something preferable out; this is a truly "scientific" American belief and hard to dislodge. The analogue of the baseball pitcher is useful in refuting it. Students can often see that the pitcher's mastery of different kinds of curves, his control of speed, and even his tactics and strategy do not take up space in his head. If a teacher tells his pupils that the human mind is more like a big-league pitcher than a block of pigeonholes, they will sometimes for the nonce believe him. They will still have a hankering after specialization to be fostered by their other teachers, and the man who has just demonstrated his hatred of any such thing will be described as a specialist.

Among the first things I learned as a preceptor was the power of continuity to awaken and hold interest. Because days and sometimes weeks intervened between conferences with a student, there was a temptation to turn the page and start anew, but I discovered that doing this broke the line of communication. It is good to carry forward a subject of contemplation and discussion, establish its relations, and, if possible, provide the basis for a comprehensive view at the end. In any case, some sort of continuity is necessary. It may not amount to dramatic suspense, but it is suspense, and the mind is so constituted that it demands a sense of progress and construction. Something must, after all, be charged against a serious purpose on the part of the student, and some day college professors will realize and admit that they lack the glamour of movie stars and public entertainers.

Connected with this is another related notion, namely, that it is a mistake to pretend that everything is easy when it is not. I believe that, by and large, it is better to tell students that some subjects are not easy to master. Such a policy is not only more honest but more inspiring than an unrealistic one. William James has some very useful comments in his chapters on "Attention" and "Association" in the first volume of *The Principles of Psychology,* and on "Will" in the second. In the former it is explained that those parts of an object or event that possess interest resist the inevitable tendency towards decay and corrosion in the mind, and there is no other preservative known. It seems paradoxical that Wilson continually inveighed against knowledge as such while he himself burned the midnight oil to obtain knowledge and plainly recognized that its acquisition was necessary for the comprehension of *meaning,* which he regarded as the end and purpose of study. Was he thinking about the storing up of unrelated facts, the sort of thing that breeds wonder in quizzes? If so, there is little cause for disagreement, and my insistence on continuity would be better described as "relatedness."

James's chapter on "Will" by inference presents a crucial issue: shall we teach or shall we learn? Will is on the side of learning, as it is also on the side of conduct and morals. It favors the real thing and despises the idea of "getting by." I should like to believe that we might create a system by means of which we could put the American college student on an assembly line and pass him along, adding wheels, engine, nuts and bolts, body, interior fittings, and paint, so that he would finally roll off on commencement day a model of style and convenience; but it cannot be done. There are, I think, no *a priori* young Americans. At least Wilson thought there should be none.

My difficulty was and is indifference and how to meet it. We literary people are not the only ones who suffer. The whole group of arts and sciences encounter the same obstruction. Whenever they leave the narrow field of the practical, the realm of *cui bono,* their followers grow as few as ours. I borrow a motto for this American class from Hoby's translation of Castiglione's *Courtier:* "I will not know the thing that toucheth me not." I believe that the class is permeable, and it is a chief satisfaction of my university life that I have made so many inroads on it.

I would not deprecate in the least Wilson's lofty idealism or say that it is not widely effective among college and university students, even among those who might not be expected to accept it. We preceptors were all conscious of Wilson's high ideals and were moved by them. It seems therefore appropriate to close this chapter on the preceptorial effort at Princeton with some excerpts from what is possibly Wilson's loftiest utterance on the subject—an address delivered before Phi Beta Kappa at Cambridge, Massachusetts, July 1, 1909, entitled, appropriately, "The Spirit of Learning," which reveals the spirit of a great academic adventure.

The college has been the seat of ideals. The liberal training which it sought to impart took no thought of any particular profession or business, but was meant to reflect in its few and simple disciplines the image of life and thought. Men were bred by it to no skill or craft or calling: the discipline to which they were subjected had a more general object. It was meant to prepare them for the whole of life rather than for some particular part of it. The ideals which lay at its heart were the general ideals of conduct, of right living, and right thinking, which made them aware of a world moralized by principle, steadied and cleared of many an evil thing by true and catholic reflection and just feeling, a world, not of interests, but of ideas.

We must re-examine the college, reconceive it, reorganize it. It is the root of our intellectual life as a nation. It is not only the instrumentality through which we must effect all the broad preliminary work which underlies sound scholarship; it is also our chief instrumentality of catholic enlightenment, our chief means of giving widespread stimulation to the whole intellectual life of the country and supplying ourselves with men who shall both comprehend their age and duty and know how to serve them supremely well. Without the American college our young men would be too exclusively shut in to the pursuit of individual interests, would lose the vital contacts and emulations which awaken them to those larger achievements and sacrifices which are the highest objects of education in a country of free citizens, where the welfare of the commonwealth springs out of the character and the informed purposes of the private citizen. The college will be found to lie somewhere very near the heart of American social training and intellectual and moral enlightment.

There went along with the relaxation of rule as to what undergraduates should study, therefore, an almost absolute divorce between the studies and the life of the college, its business and its actual daily occupations. The teacher ceased to look upon himself as related in any responsible way to the life of his pupils, to what they should be doing and thinking of between one class exercise and another, and conceived his whole duty to have been performed when he had given his lecture and afforded those who were appointed to come the opportunity to hear and heed it if they chose. The teachers of the new regime, moreover, were most of them trained for their teaching work in German universities, or in American universities in which the methods, the points of view, the spirit, and the object of the German universities were, consciously or unconsciously, reproduced. They think of their pupils, therefore, as men already disciplined by some general training such as the German gymnasium gives, and seeking in the university special acquaintance with particular studies, as an introduction to special fields of information and inquiry. They have never thought of the university as a community of teachers and pupils: they think of it rather as a body of teachers and investigators to whom those may resort who seriously desire specialized kinds of knowledge. They are specialists imported into an American system which has lost its old point of view and found no new one suitable to the needs and circumstances of America. They do not think of living with their pupils and affording them the contacts of culture; they are only accessible to them at stated periods and for a definite and limited service; and their teaching is an interruption of their favorite work of research.

The effects of learning are its real tests, the real tests alike of its validity and its efficacy. The mind can be driven, but that is not life. Life is voluntary or unconscious. It is breathed in out of a sustaining atmosphere. It is shaped by environment. It is habitual, continuous, productive. It does not consist in tasks performed, but in powers gained and enhanced. It cannot be communicated in classrooms if its aim and end is the classroom. Instruction is not its source, but only its incidental means and medium.

What we should seek to impart in our colleges, therefore, is not so much learning itself as the spirit of learning. You can impart that to young men; and you can impart it in the three or four years at your disposal. It consists in the power to distinguish good reasoning from bad, in the power to digest and interpret evidence, in a habit of catholic observation and a preference for the non-partisan point of view, in an addiction to clear and logical processes of thought and yet an instinctive desire to interpret rather than to stick in the letter of the reasoning, in a taste for knowledge and a deep respect for the integrity of the human mind. It is citizenship of the world of knowledge, but not ownership of it. Scholars are the owners of its varied parts, in severalty.

It [a college] should give them insight into the things of the mind and of the spirit, a sense of having lived and formed their friendships amidst the gardens of the mind where grows the tree of the knowledge of good and evil, a consciousness of having taken on them the vows of true enlightenment and of having undergone the discipline, never to be shaken off, of those who seek wisdom in candor, with faithful labour and travail of spirit.

These things they cannot get from the class-room unless the spirit of the class-room is the spirit of the place as well and of its life; and that will never be until the teacher comes out of the class-room and makes himself a part of that life. Contact, companionship, familiar intercourse is the law of life for the mind. The comradeships of undergraduates will never breed the spirit of learning. The circle must be widened. It must include the older men, the teachers, the men for whom life has grown more serious and to whom it has revealed more of its meanings. So long as instruction and life do not merge in our colleges, so long as what the undergraduates do and what they are taught occupy two separate, air-tight compartments in their consciousness, so long will the college be ineffectual.

It is the duty of university authorities to make of the college a society, of which the teacher will be as much, and as naturally, a member as the undergraduate. When that is done other things will fall into their natural places, their natural relations. Young men are capable of great enthusiasms for older men whom they have learned to know in some human, unartificial way, whose quality they have tasted in unconstrained conversation, the energy and beauty of whose characters and aims they have learned to appreciate by personal contact; and such enthusiasms are often among the strongest and most lasting influences of their lives. You will not gain the affection of your pupil by anything you do for him, impersonally, in the class-room. You may gain his admiration and vague appreciation, but he will tie to you only for what you have shown him personally or given him in intimate and friendly service.

Do that; create the atmosphere and the contacts of a society made up of men young and old, mature and adolescent, serious and gay, and you will create an emulation, a saturation, a vital union of parts in a common life, in which all questions of subordination and proportion will solve themselves.

My plea, then, is this: that we now deliberately set ourselves to make a home for the spirit of learning: that we reorganize our colleges on the lines of this simple conception, that a college is not only a body of studies but a mode of association; that its courses are only its formal side, its contacts and contagions its realities. It must become a community of scholars and pupils,—a free community but a very real one, in which democracy may work its reasonable triumphs of accommodation, its vital processes of union. I am not suggesting that young men be dragooned into becoming scholars or tempted to become pedants, or have any artificial compulsion whatever put upon them, but only that they be introduced into the high society of university ideals, be exposed to the hazards of stimulating friendships, be introduced into the easy comradeships of the republic of letters. By this means the class-room itself might some day come to seem a part of life.

In this address, Wilson had in mind not only the small, independent college or the collegiate aspect and function of a university, but also and primarily an ideal academic community that never was on sea or land. Not even Solomon's House, except in the pursuit of truth through investigation, fulfills his ideal. But in the Princeton experiment and in other community efforts there have been approximations of what cultivated people might do if they would. I cannot help suggesting that in "The Spirit of Learning," Wilson in some distant way draws an idealized picture of McCosh's Princeton as it was from 1875 to 1879, when Wilson was an undergraduate. Many of the features he terms essential were present in Princeton's academic life at that time. The college was small enough to find unity of spirit in a great, learned, and humane leader and in a faculty that seems to have been kindly and competent and to have seen eye to eye with McCosh. There is every evidence that religion was a strongly unifying force, a rather stern religion in its insistence on righteous conduct, harmony with one's fellows, and a sense of responsibility and duty. As we know, the student body came from respectable American families and had experienced pretty much the same up-bringing. These students must have been comparatively undisturbed by sharp differences in wealth and social aspirations. The institution was relatively poor, and its creed allowed for humility and diligence. That seemed the only way in those days of prospering and winning distinction, and Princeton wanted both prosperity and distinction. Princeton had no outstanding academic importance, and the life and control of the college must have been simpler than it is now.

In this connection I am somehow reminded of a reply from the president of a small, respectable southern college on a questionnaire I had sent out in the course of preparing a report for the American Association of University Professors on faculty participation in appointments and promotions. The question was: "When your institution receives a donation, is your faculty consulted about the expenditure of the funds?" The president's answer: "We don't have too much money at this place, and, when we get any, we all put our heads together and see how far we can make it go."

Wilson had had trying experiences, when he wrote this Phi Beta Kappa address, with the encroachment of the community and of special interests on the university in matters that he deemed affairs of the university itself, and it is not hard to find in the turn of his phrases a slight undercurrent of disappointment and even a tendency to take refuge, as we all do, in the impeccable ideal. The last time I heard him speak was at the University of Minnesota during the presidential campaign of 1912—a nonpolitical address. On that occasion he took a rather somber view of the American university in its function of serving the state. In "The Spirit of Learning," he does not despair, but is bolstered by a feeling of satisfaction in what he has done at Princeton to set the course of study in proper order and to unite faculty and students in a common enterprise. Indeed, I think that at that time Princeton closely approximated his ideal conception of an academic institution unified by a spirit of intellectual interest and effort.

The effect of the preceptorial system and its accompanying changes was not only powerful but lasting. It was not that the proportional number of students of the very highest quality was greatly increased. *"Vixere fortes ante Agamemnona."* What happened was a rise in the general level of scholarship. Students of mediocre performance were fewer, and proportional grading grew absurd. "B-grade" students tripled in numbers and proportion. Thoughtful cognizance of issues and independent and largely self-directed investigation became customary and expected. One year, I have forgotten which one, some eighty students were flunked out. There is nothing extraordinary about that, for the method was new and students did not know how to follow it. The unusual thing is that the whole lot came back to finish their courses, for they knew what was good for them, so to speak, what they needed. This trend continued to the very end of my period of service, so that at the time the gods and the demigods were belaboring one another in the sky, Princeton students were going quietly and steadily on their way. I later went west with the idea that I should find a prevalence of students poorly trained, perhaps, but aspiring to great accomplishment in their lives. I have indeed met with many students of high ambition and energy, but nowhere since I left Princeton have I found anything comparable to what it possessed. I do not mean spectacular talent, I mean plain things: personal ambition, high moral ideals, and willingness to work.

CHAPTER V

Counterrevolution

IN THE SPRING of 1907, at Murray Hall, I happened to see what may have been the practical beginning of Wilson's project for the establishment of a house system at Princeton. I shall avoid as far as possible the use of the word "quad." A meeting was being held to settle some particularly outrageous violation of the upper-class club treaty, and the group included Wilson and Hibben. In the center of the group was a gigantic football hero bawling like a calf, whether in contrition for his own sins and those of his fellow club members or for the sins of others I do not know. There he was, and Wilson's face looked very serious.

At any rate, I had never heard of a plan for a house system to replace the upper-class clubs until after that great, or pseudogreat, scandal, and after that the matter became one of general interest and frequent discussion. It sickens me to remember that one historian represents the enterprise as a dark, secret plot suddenly sprung upon a body of unsuspecting and innocent undergraduates. Wilson talked with me about it, and I heard him talk at greater length with others, once with the undergraduates. It was presented as a plan for the betterment of Princeton life and was freely discussed and argued. Most, if not all, of the people I associated with thought it a step in the right direction, and it was certainly presented as a matter to be worked on and thought about. The fact that Princeton's confidence in Wilson was at an acme had considerable bearing on the genesis and fate of the plan.

The major document preserved regarding the original plan is Wilson's "Report on the Social Co-ordination of the University," submitted to the trustees on June 10, 1907. The following excerpts from it merit careful consideration. Wilson describes the successful operation of the preceptorial system and then turns his attention to the corresponding social environment:

Undoubtedly, if we would give Princeton the highest distinction and that academic leadership in the country she may now so easily gain, we must study at every turn the means by which to lift her intellectual achievements out of mediocrity not only, but also into such an order of naturalness and energy and distinction as shall make her by reason of her way of success a conspicuous model and example. There is no true intellectual life for the undergraduate in the mere faithful performance of set tasks, no matter how eagerly or with what concentration he devotes himself to them, if between tasks his mind be emptied of the interest they have created and his life run entirely free of their influence. There must somehow be brought about an interpenetration of his experience inside the class room and conference and his experience outside academic exercises, where men register their interests by what they do and say and let their minds have play upon.

Princeton had never been a true residential college, continued Wilson, for it had furnished only sleeping quarters and had never provided for meals and recreation, which consequently the students had supplied by establishing their own select eating clubs.

Counterrevolution

The evident peculiarity of this life is that it severs the social from the intellectual interests of the place, and does not, with its scattered clubs and divided classes, make us up into a community even on the social side. The vital units are the club units. They divide all four classes into segments and sharply separate the classes as wholes from one another during the two earlier years of the undergraduate course, when characters are being formed and points of view established. The organization is entirely outside university action; has no organic connection whatever with anything academic; produces interests which absorb the attention and the energy of the best undergraduates as of all others, and yet nowhere interpenetrates the associations which arise out of study, carries no flavour with it which it might not as well have in any other town or in any other similar environment.

It absorbs the attention and all the planning faculties of the undergraduates because all social ambitions turn upon it. It would be difficult to exaggerate the importance in the life of the undergraduate of the question whether at the end of his Sophomore year he is going to be taken into one of the upper-class clubs. His thought is constantly fixed upon that object throughout the first two years of his university course with a great intensity and uneasiness whenever he thinks either of his social standing, his comradeships, or his general social consideration among his fellows. The clubs do not take in all members of the Junior and Senior classes. About one-third are left out in the elections; and their lot is little less than deplorable. They feel that they cannot continue to associate on terms of intimacy with friends who have been elected into clubs, for fear they will be thought to be seeking to make favour with them and obtain a belated invitation to join; and even, when many of them as individuals are not disappointed at having been passed by, they must seek their comradeships with other classmates who are very much disappointed and who feel their isolation with a good deal of bitterness. It is difficult for them to arrange for comfortable eating places; and the places at which they do board are only too much like caves of Adullam. They go forward to their graduation almost like men who are in the University and yet not of it. Often, they are cheerful and steadfast enough; individuals here and there are sometimes quite indifferent to their comparative isolation, being absorbed in their books or in the task of earning the money necessary to pay their college expenses, but as a class their position is most trying. It often happens that men who fail of election to one of the clubs at the end of the Sophomore year leave the University and go to some other college or abandon altogether the idea of completing their university course.

So soon as the practice threatened to grow up of seeking out attractive and especially desirable under-classmen and pledging them in advance to accept elections into particular upper-class clubs, a treaty of the most stringent character was entered into by the clubs which sought to make it an act of personal dishonour on the part of any upper-classman who was a member of a club to cultivate relations of personal intimacy with under-classmen for fear such ends might be in view. The treaty has again and again been violated, and again and again renewed, in stricter and stricter form, until, in its present shape, as now pending for readoption, it practically seeks to fix an impassable gulf between the upper and lower classes in order that such attempts and suspicions may be altogether avoided.

Two very significant and very undesirable, and even dangerous, things have thus come about: the two lower classes, who need above all things the forming, guiding influence of the upper-classes, have been almost completely segregated, and the very influences which seemed to render their segregation necessary from the point of view of the clubmen have brought about the very result their segregation was meant to prevent, that is, they have cut them up into groups and cliques whose social ambitions give them separate and rival interests quite distinct from, plainly hostile to, the interests of the University as a whole.

116

Along with the steadily increasing concentration of the attention of the undergraduates upon the social question and the centering of all social ambitions upon the upper-class clubs has gone a very noticeable, a very rapid, increase in the luxury of the upper-class clubhouses. The two oldest clubs now have houses of extraordinary elegance and luxury of appointment and five other clubs are maturing plans for replacing their present comfortable structures with buildings which will rival the others in beauty, spaciousness, and comfort. The University which gives life to these clubs and constitutes their ostensible *raison d'être,* seems in danger of becoming, if the present tendencies of undergraduate organization are allowed to work out their logical results, only an artistic setting and background for life on Prospect Avenue. That life, as it becomes more and more elaborate, will become more and more absorbing, and university interests will fall more and more into the background. The interest of the lower classes will more and more centre upon it and the energies of the upper classes will be more and more engrossed by it. The vital life of the place will be outside the University and in large part independent of it.

Before the establishment of the preceptorial system, with its necessary corollary of the intimate association of teacher and pupil,—the co-ordination of the undergraduate life with the teaching of the University,—these things were not so near the heart of our plans and hopes for Princeton's intellectual development and academic revitalization. But now they are the essence of everything we are striving for, whether on the undergraduate or on the graduate side of the University's work, and we are bound to consider the means by which to effect an immediate change of our undergraduate life.

Your committee is of the opinion that the only adequate means of accomplishing this is the grouping of the undergraduates in residential quadrangles, each with its common dining hall, its common room for intercourse and diversion, and its resident masters and preceptors; where members of all four classes shall be associated in a sort of family life, not merely as neighbors in dormitories but as comrades at meals and in many daily activities,—the upper classes ruling and forming the lower, and all in constant association with members of the Faculty fitted to act in sympathetic co-operation with them in the management of their common life. In brief, your Committee is of the opinion that the only way in which the social life of the undergraduates can be prevented from fatally disordering, and perhaps even strangling, the academic life of the University is by the actual absorption of the social life into the academic.

This is not the scheme of the English colleges. Those colleges have separate autonomy. Each separately undertakes the instruction of the undergraduates resident within it. The plan we propose involves only a convenient residential division of the University as a social body.

The effect of this plan upon the upper-class clubs would be either their abolition or their absorption. The withdrawal of the greater part of the Juniors and Seniors from the life of the proposed residential quads would of course be out of the question. A separate club life for them would rob the whole plan of its vitality, and is not to be thought of. But the history of the upper-class clubs has been most honourable and useful. They have served the University in a period of transition, when no plans were thought of for its co-ordination, as perhaps no other instrumentalities could have served it. Their abolition ought not to be thought of if their adaptation to the new order of things can be effected. It would be a violent breach of historical continuity and out of tone with the traditions and standards of growth which have hitherto kept Princeton intact as an organic whole. Fortunately, if we should be happy enough to secure their co-operation, it will be quite possible to develop them into smaller residential quads as part of the University itself; and this, in the opinion of your Committee, would be the happiest possible solution of the difficulty, giving to clubs which are now in danger of embarrassing and even profoundly demoralizing the life of the University a role of singular distinction and public spirit in its organic development, and affording the country at large a new example of Princeton's capacity to lead the way in matters of organization which are now puzzling the authorities of all our larger universities. We can lead in social example. And our alumni and undergraduates will, as usual, be our partners in the enterprise.[1]

Wilson then asks that authority be granted the administration to take such steps as may seem wisest for maturing this general plan and for seeking the co-operation and counsel of the upper-class clubs in its elaboration.

The report, which shows by its style that it is from Wilson's own hand, was possibly his masterpiece to that date in the art of persuasion, to which he had devoted much thought and effort in earlier life. It will be noted that it has nothing to say about the "democratization" of Princeton, but seems to imply that, although the democracy of Princeton life was threatened, there was still time to preserve it. Later statements by Wilson may indicate a change of attitude, but in this report there is no evidence of anything but good will. It dwells on the ills that regularly attended the election of sophomores to upper-class clubs, asserting that great evils in the enforced segregation of classes had already been perpetrated and deprecating the strain placed upon underclassmen by the system of choice, certainly one of the worst systems on record. The report has nothing to say about changing that system, but proposes an organization of houses so inclusive as to make the clubs, as such, undesirable. It does not attack the clubs or accuse them of any misconduct. It puts stress on the desirability of association among the university classes for the sake of the influence of the older men upon the

[1] *Public Papers*, I, 499–521.

younger men. Wilson once told me that he so looked up to those who were seniors when he was a freshman that members of the class of 1876 still, in his imagination, walked about with halos on their heads.

The report puts the whole stress on the obstruction offered by the social system as it existed to the ideal life of learning and study. It argues that absorption in social life had for many students taken the place of education. Wilson was convinced that "the sideshow had swallowed the circus," or was about to do so. Social obsession had made it impossible for Princeton students to live a life of study and thought, discussion and exchange. The report argues this point strongly and shrewdly.

Wilson may have been right. In the long run he was certainly so, but, considering the question locally and immediately, I thought the ability of active young men to be vividly interested in a variety of things was underestimated and that, in any case, Princeton students were attending to their studies more effectively than I had ever seen it done before. Of course I was merely a teacher and an obscure one, and it was not for me to plan the future of Princeton. I saw difficulties, mainly organizational, in the way, but difficulties were merely things to be overcome, and I accepted outright Wilson's plan for building the greatest possible Princeton.

Wilson's plan was freely discussed by students in their relatively irresponsible way with a frankness that has not been noted. I was in a position to overhear many of their debates, formal and informal. I recall two opposing speeches, both of which made use of Wilson's own words. One speaker repeated an idea I think he had gotten from me. Democracy, Wilson had said, is a positive force that demands its rights, sometimes rudely, because it is entitled to them and will not accept as favors from rulers the things that are its own. The speaker went on to say that, if the function of Princeton was to train its graduates for the service of the state, it had no right to countenance and to maintain on its campus a system of privilege for one set of its students to which other students might not be admitted, whatever their deserts might be.

His opponent quoted Wilson to the effect that the perfect democrat and the perfect aristocrat are almost indistinguishable in their social outlook and conduct. The former is so just in character that he will insist that every man have his equal share, and the latter so enlightened, so generous, so sympathetic with his fellow men that no man will suffer at his hands, but all will profit by his magnanimity. Therefore, the debater argued, both social justice and the general welfare lay in the hands of the aristocrats. Princeton had specialized in the production of such men and should continue to do so. To me the question was wide open and assumed the form of what was the best road to real greatness for Princeton.

My conviction that this matter was subject to free discussion rests not only on what I heard and saw but also on what I think was the truth about Wilson. He was a lifelong believer in the voice of an enlightened majority. "Taking counsel" and "the meeting of minds" were his favorite phrases —and practices. He was extremely careful in arriving at principles and, as I have said, was pre-eminent in his ability to be right. Wilson was infinitely polite and considerate in his dealings with people, and he listened to what they said. He made many concessions—I thought he made too many— and agreed to changes in his plans. When he thought his opposition was factious, his attitude hardened. He knew the difficulties of carrying out his proposal to reorganize the life of the undergraduates, expected that changes and adjustments would need to be made, and intended that all practical details of institution and operation be carried out along lines of justice and reason. His letter to the presidents of the upper-class clubs shows these features and principles:

The objects of this arrangement would be: (1) To place unmarried members of the Faculty in residence in the quads in order to bring them into close, habitual, natural association with the undergraduates and so intimately tie the intellectual and social life of the place into one another; (2) to associate the four classes in a genuinely organized manner and make of the University a real social body, to the exclusion of cliques and separate class social organizations; (3) to give to the University the kind of common consciousness which apparently comes from the closer sorts of social contact, to be had only outside the classroom, and most easily to be got about a common table, and in the contacts of a common life.

The details of the adjustments which would be necessary I have in large part thought out; but I do not wish to dwell upon them now, simply because I wish them to be subject to change in my own mind. These complicated things cannot be wisely planned or executed except by the slow processes of common counsel; and I should wish the details of such a scheme of transformation to be worked out by the frank conference of all concerned.

But some things seem to be clear. I should hope that, in effecting the transition, each club would vest its property in the hands of a small board of trustees of its own choice who would be charged with administering it for the benefit of the University in association of the present university authorities; and that that board should have important powers of advice or confirmation in respect of the appointment of resident members of the Faculty and the regulations governing the assignment of students to the quad under its supervision, and with regard to all matters upon which they could retain a hold without embarrassing the uniform government of the University or the supreme authority of the Trustees of the University itself. And I see no reason why the graduate members of the several clubs might not retain all the privileges they now enjoy in respect to the use of the club and meals at the club tables on their visits to Princeton.

I see no reason why they should ever feel their relations to the clubs at all radically altered because the clubs had in effect become residential colleges.[2]

Wilson's hypothetical picture of the situation at the end of his letter is perfectly plausible—merely that of an Oxford college, say at Eights Week, when alumni and families of the students visit the college. I think there is no reasonable doubt that Wilson thought at that time that the transition would be a long and difficult one and that he was too wise to be definite. It is plain that he expected and desired discussion and advice. I can sympathize with those who want the institutions of their youth to remain exactly as they were, but I recognize the futility of their wishes. Things, including colleges, never remain static. Princeton has changed and will continue to change, and it might, or it might not, take some action generally in line with Wilson's principles; but, as it stands, the plan is a mere matter of history and belongs to the realm of what might have been—if the South had won its independence, if a musket ball had destroyed Napoleon on the bridge at Lodi, what you will—but let us be just and, as far as we can, truthful. Wilson told me and no doubt others that he was surprised at the unanimity with which his proposal for the social co-ordination of the University was accepted by the board of trustees.

It must, therefore, have been a trying experience to meet the rejection of that same proposal at a subsequent meeting of the board in the following autumn. He described the meeting to me: The board assembled, and, after attending to certain routine business, one member moved that the resolution adopted on June 10, 1907, be reconsidered. Wilson welcomed the resolution to reconsider because he wanted discussion and advice. He was surprised and, it must be said,

[2] *Ibid.,* 518–21.

offended, when, after the adoption of the motion, the board sat in stony silence and refused to argue or explain their position, although the proposal was again before the assembly and debate was in order. Wilson felt this was an insult to his whole career and to his sincerity of character as a man and a citizen. It is not for me to account for the reversal of attitude on the part of the trustees or for their silence, and I could not do so if I would. It is easy to say that during the summer, while Wilson was in England, the good trustees had had time to think deeply and pray earnestly about the issue, but there is no evidence to that effect. It is equally easy to ask with Parolles, "Who cannot be crushed with a plot?" Baker thinks the reversal resulted in part from West's and Cleveland's determination that the graduate college rank first on the program, and he may be, at least in part, right.

My interest in Wilson's proposal long ago dwindled to thoughts about its ideals, immediate and remote, and to speculation, not too hopeful, about whether the colossal university world will ever espouse and put into practice his ideal, which was essentially the perfection and perpetuation of American democracy.

Even in those days—they stretched over two or three years —I was never particularly sympathetic with those youths who were vaguely reported to have been rejected for membership in the upper-class clubs and so left the university with broken hearts and presumably pined away and died. Those Princeton plants seemed too spindly to be worth saving. My friends among the students, who were mostly reading men, were made of sterner stuff. There was no one of them, I think, who would not have had the manliness to tell his rejecters to go to hell and then go on about the business of making an efficient citizen of himself. I was also not greatly moved by the effeminate idea of creating so many clubs that every Princeton man might belong to one.

This lack of social sympathy is possibly a fault in me, but there has been so much that could be and should be done to educate the American youth that I have lacked the time to cultivate my sweeter sentiments; yet I would not be inconsiderate. The rich we have with us always, and we must not be lacking in charity. Their youth and often the youth of their hangers-on have little chance to know the happiness there is in service and individual achievement. It is perhaps no wonder that memberships, baubles, and luxury have exaggerated value in their eyes.

There is no doubt that Wilson believed in democracy and that he believed there were undemocratic elements in the life at Princeton and other American seats of learning. I know that that proposition has been denied, but it does not serve my purpose to argue the truth of the matter, since my immediate interest is in what Wilson thought about universities. He undoubtedly felt also that engrossing social interests were interfering seriously with the real purpose of the university. In a letter of February 1, 1910, he writes, "My ideals for the University are those of genuine democracy and serious scholarship. The two, indeed, seem to me to go together. Any organization which introduces elements of social exclusiveness constitutes the worst possible soil for serious intellectual endeavor." There is nothing noncommittal about that. He says again in an address at the inauguration of the president of Franklin and Marshall College, January 10, 1910, "College life in our day has become so absorbing a thing that college work has fallen into the background." But he would not be unreasonable about it, as appears in an address before the Princeton Club of Chicago, March 12, 1908:

After all, gentlemen, a University has as its only legitimate object intellectual attainment. I do not mean that there should not go along with that a great deal that is delightful in the way of comradeship; but I am sure that men never thoroughly enjoy each other if they merely touch superficially. I do not believe that men ever thoroughly know and enjoy each other until they lay their minds alongside each other and make real test of their quality.[3]

These opinions were not new with Wilson—he had held them all his mature life—and can anybody who has had college experience deny their general truth? Have we not had thrust upon us for fifty years the banal statement that one attends college to learn to make friends and influence people? Have we not seen students preferred and praised for devoting their time to extracurricular activities, because these things, we have been told, are more important than the education that might come from the pursuit of knowledge? And is it not known and acknowledged that co-educational institutions are to be preferred because of the matrimonial opportunities they afford? The cruel snobbishness of the young about membership in clubs, societies, and fraternities becomes slightly less important when viewed as merely another enemy of American university education. Baker's description of Wilson's general attitude may, I think, be accepted as sound:

Wilson felt, in suggesting this remedy, that he was asking nothing revolutionary. He was merely recognizing one of the more or less natural and instinctive efforts of the students to counterbalance the huge numerical growth of American universities—common to all of them—by setting up manageable units of the spirit to replace the small college with its closer associations. Wilson was proposing to take these clubs, which were not evil in themselves, and convert them into colleges within the university—thus utilizing their benefits and at the same time robbing them of the features

3 *Princeton Alumni Weekly,* Vol. VIII (1908), 402–505.

which made them undesirable—the privilege, the exclusiveness, the rivalries, the luxury. His idea at this time was that the change would be neither expensive nor very difficult.[4]

When Wilson said, "The changes necessary to effect the transition would be, in form at any rate, very slight," he was relying, as Baker indirectly suggests, on the devotion and loyalty of both students and alumni, and I think, as I remember the situation, that Wilson was possibly right with reference to the ease with which his plan might have gone through. The opposition came not from the students or faculty but from outside forces, an opposition that multiplied and strengthened the obstacles in the way of the plan. Money was certainly a stumbling block. Had Wilson had only students and faculty to deal with and funds at his disposal, the college plan might conceivably have gone into effect. I took little interest in the battle that ensued, indeed was annoyed by it, for, as I have remarked, Princeton seemed to me to be in an admirable state intellectually. In any case, Wilson, in his hope to set an example to the universities of the country, did suggest a rational method of procedure in dealing with the social organization of university students. Its likeness to the English system testifies to its workability.

So far as I know, no great headway has been made towards the democratization of American university life. Universities have grown richer and now have everywhere groups of students who are at least applying the principle of exclusiveness, which, I take it, is a bastard form of aristocracy. These groups would be worse than they are but for the overwhelming number of independent students who discount their pretensions and diminish their importance. Certainly, Wilson's plan was simple, educational, and unwarped by political bias. There are enough "ordinary fellows" about to profit by such an

4 *Life and Letters*, II, 221.

organization, which would quicken and mature the intellectual life of universities. In his letter to Andrew C. Imbrie, July 29, 1907, Wilson seems well aware of the general import of his recommendation:

As for myself, I feel that we are here debating, not only a plan but an opportunity to solve a question common to all the colleges and obtain a leadership which will not be in our choice to get again within our lifetime. The colleges of the country are looking to us for leadership in this matter, as in others, and if we disappoint them it will be an opportunity irretrievably lost. I have talked this subject over with a great many men from other universities, and I feel convinced that our solution will be accepted as the general solution, if we have strength and courage to act upon it.

The experiments in the use of the house plan that I have seen in operation or heard described are praiseworthy and no doubt socially valuable, but so far they seem to lack the integration of Wilson's scheme, which had as its foundation actually joint participation of faculty and students in the interests and activities of learning and study. I think so well of Wilson's scheme as an educational device that I should like to see it given a trial, although I think its effectiveness would be greatly increased if the university at which it was instituted had a curriculum that took into account the *a posteriori* nature of discursive studies and was arranged to include broader courses of study than are presently offered.

I have no wish to re-create the unpleasant atmosphere of 1907-1908, but rather to confirm the importance of Wilson's scheme by quoting an ironical passage from his address before the Princeton Club of Chicago, March 12, 1908:

Looking back upon these years it seems to me a very interesting circumstance, gentlemen, that when we revolution-

128

ized the course of study at Princeton and absolutely changed
the method of instruction, it raised hardly a ripple upon the
surface of the alumni.

They were interested when they heard that things had
been done that were considered noteworthy; they were grati-
fied; but in accepting what had been done evidently thought
of it as a purely intellectual matter and entirely our business.
But when we came to touching the social life of the University, that was another matter; not a ripple of excitement, not
a mere ripple of excitement, but a storm of excitement swept
the body academic, and we know that we had at last touched
the vital matter.

In the now partly lost address before the Princeton Club
of Pittsburgh, April 16, 1910, Wilson makes a disturbing
evaluation of the college situation in our country:

> While attending a recent Lincoln celebration I asked my-
> self if Lincoln would have been as serviceable to the people
> of this country, had he been a college man, and I was obliged
> to say to myself that he would not. The process to which the
> college man is subjected does not render him serviceable to
> the country as a whole. It is for this reason that I have dedi-
> cated every power in me to a democratic regeneration.[5]

From the point of view of university education it is useless
to dwell on the defeat of Wilson's plan of reform and on the
men who supported it and opposed it and the reasons why
they did so, but it is important for the modern world to
know and think about the principles at its base, for the work
is yet to be done. It is worse than stupid for historians to
twist the proposal and its maker out of focus for what seem
to be no reasons at all. The proposal to democratize American universities either has merit or it has not, but certainly,
as a means of integrating the lives and the studies of univer-

[5] *Public Papers*, II, 202–203.

sity students, the proposed device deserves respectful consideration.

In so far as the democratization of university life means inducing university and college men to be willing and eager to serve their country and not merely themselves, there can be no exception taken. If it means an attack on special privileges within a public institution, there seems to be a difference of opinion, although I see no reason why in the United States there should be. Let us not think of it as a lost cause. American universities are not as supine as their behavior sometimes indicates. For example, the ideal of serving the ordinary student so well that he does not need membership in special groups for either comfort or comradeship, an ideal not unknown at Stanford, is worth considering, and that fundamentally was Wilson's goal. Princeton's age-old command, "Thou shalt have no other gods before me," would be becomingly expressed in such a policy.

The idea, which appeared at Princeton in my time, that we academicians were greatly in need of social and academic refinement was offensive to me from the start. I think I was at fault, but I was not properly impressed with academic ceremonies, costumes, and customs, although I had been for a short time a student in Germany and was a member of an Oxford college. I had seen something of the way things were done in ancient institutions. I had dined in hall a good many times, bowed my head when a Latin grace was said, and knew in which direction to pass the port. I admired Tudor architecture and Duke Humphrey's remarkable Bodleian Library, but did most of my work in the Radcliffe Camera, its reading room. I was not convinced, as perhaps I should have been, of our rurality and of our need to be more ceremonious and luxurious, but I behaved as properly as I could and was much pleased to be at Princeton.

A few years after I took my degree, Dean West, with his

fine artistic sense and his admiration for refined and orderly living, began with the assistance of Professor Butler his movement for the creation of a finer life for postgraduate students. This movement was initiated at Merwick, and I am sure was most successful. Throughout the rest of my career at Princeton there was a steady and efficient pressure for the building of a great residential college for these young scholars, conceived on rather magnificent lines and intended to carry out the ideals for scholastic living and learning that West espoused. It seemed to me, and to others, unnecessarily sumptuous and not absolutely essential to the training of American scholars and university professors. This is not to say that there was anything frivolous or superficial in Dean West's plan, for, in point of fact, his standards of scholarship were very high. I merely give my opinion to warn the reader that I may be unintentionally a prejudiced witness in the case now before us—the last great university episode in my Princeton career.

Great fights have a way of being always at the barriers. John Cotton and Roger Williams debated religious toleration in terms of the proper exegesis of the parable of the tares in the wheat, and I think the great controversy at Princeton about the graduate college did not concern postgraduate study but sundry matters of power, immediate and remote, and political and social issues. I am not interested in these issues at this time, for I doubt that they are fundamental. There were, however, questions in two or three parts that did pertain to postgraduate study as such, and these I shall discuss.

One quite definite ideal for graduate study came to prevail at Princeton during my time and, I judge, still prevails in the older eastern universities of the United States. There is much to be said for it. It began with a properly trained college graduate and ended with a doctor of philosophy who had maturity—personally, socially, and academically. Such a person had had time to read and think, his environment had been orderly and, as far as possible, refined in its appointments, and his scholarship was thorough and integrated, not raw and fragmentary. He knew his foreign languages and frequently had visited foreign countries as traveler, student, and observer. In American practice it would probably be said that he had been trained for college and university teaching, but it is obvious that the education of this young scholar would also be admirable for a man of letters who is not a teacher, for the kind of private scholar that has been produced often and successfully in England, or for an editor, publisher, reviewer, or critic.

There was a belief at Princeton, which I think is still held in some cultural centers in the East, that for the welfare of our country and of civilization men who were being trained to teach in the West and South should as far as possible be prepared to represent the highest academic, social, and individual refinement. It was thought that these regions were in need of cultural refinement, and I agree, but at the same time suggest that this extremely low opinion of our culture was in some measure based on ignorance. The West is no longer a primitive frontier, and standards of living are high, even luxurious. Most western and southern universities and colleges are well equipped with libraries and laboratories, and have their share of important scholars on their faculties. Further, attending colleges and universities is possibly a more general practice there than in the East itself. Institutions of higher learning in the West and South are not necessarily new, many of them being one hundred years or more old, and even the land-grant colleges will begin to celebrate their centennials in about twenty years. It is absurd and sometimes not even accurate to call attention to the fact that a majority of teachers in their faculties are still eastern or foreign trained, presupposing that such training is vital. The desire to help us on the ground that our need is great is commendable, but I doubt that our condition warrants shaping policies of graduate instruction around it. I have in mind that almost archaic report of a "committee of fifteen" issued recently that attempted to formulate a policy and practice for American graduate training. Excellent and sound ideas underlay Dean West's plan to make Princeton a cultural center; but, just as a matter of peace and harmony, I wish eastern scholars would stick to their principles and not issue reports whose substance is not their excellence but our defects.

The ideal of a protracted education for college and university professors and for everybody in the best cultural surroundings, with guidance and comradeship in learning, is a distinguished ideal. It commends itself to us by the example of the greatest scholars we have known and by the history of scholarship in the Middle Ages, the Renaissance, and modern times. Scholars of all ages have acquired a reputation for being retired, judicious, industrious, and wise.

But high scholarship is not completely dependent on wealth, leisure, or even educational advantages. Ultimately scholarship must depend on intelligence and industry, and I honestly believe that able, ambitious students can overcome serious difficulties, such as deficient early schooling, especially in foreign languages and the correct and artistic use of the English language, and limited means. I think such students should have an opportunity to try, and I myself can bear witness to many gratifying successes.

In recent years there has been an interesting development in the universities of the West and South, a development that has immediate bearing on the training of college and university teachers in the United States. It is in fact a union of teaching and scholarly study. Young men come to the universities with varied training but rather uniform lack of funds. They not infrequently have wives and children. Whatever advantages may arise from their situation, leisure is not one of them. They often have to work night and day. A sort of pattern has evolved. These young men come to the university as graduates of colleges or universities and manage to stick it out for a year and get a master's degree. If they have done superior work and want to continue their studies, they are made assistants in university instruction. Many of them are already experienced teachers, but, in any case, they are closely supervised and must do an acceptable job of teaching. They also pursue graduate studies, and in both occupations must usually satisfy rather severe standards. They have to use their minds all the time, but, really, it does not hurt a mind to use it. To meet residence requirements, prepare for and pass qualifying and comprehensive examinations, and prepare an acceptable thesis takes a long time, so that these graduate students have at least a protracted university experience. In addition, there are those who, in order to support themselves and their families, work also at various jobs in the community, sometimes at night. Many of them succeed surprisingly well, but they have to have grit.

Although one may wonder why they undertake such a difficult life, he need not waste sympathy on them. When they get through, they have learned a profession, acquired something of the dignity and independence of scholarship, and met hardships face to face. It takes both ability and character to carry through successfully such an undertaking, and, although there may be in some cases a lack of the gentility of more luxurious society, these men and their wives have become acquainted with refined people and have lived in an atmosphere of kindly culture. They have good manners, serious purpose, and often a lot of practical wisdom. I am quite willing to trust the future of American college and university students to such hands. This form and experience of education does not derogate from the merits of those who have sought excellence under more favorable circumstances, but it does deny the all too common American attitude of, "There is only one way to proceed, and that's my way."

Very roughly speaking, one may say that West would have been sympathetic towards the first of these concepts of graduate training and Wilson towards the second, although we may be perfectly sure that both men would have repudiated the opinions attributed to them, if they had been presented in this exaggerated fashion. Wilson was a steady believer in and practitioner of the amenities of university life, and West was a firm believer in hard work and genuine scholarship.

One aspect of learning while teaching has a bearing on the Princeton situation as it was in the first decade of this century. Woodrow Wilson, in recommending the plan for residential colleges, made a point of insisting on the great value of having students of different degrees of advancement associate with one another. He thought it a splendid idea for freshmen and sophomores to have the opportunity to know and associate with juniors and seniors, and brought up the same argument of mingling different levels in his advocacy of locating the graduate college in the heart of the university. I have always believed in the pleasure and utility of this practice, for I had the advantage of having my early schooling in a country schoolhouse. The older boys actually taught me more than the teachers did. They were very kind to the little boy in their midst, and listening to their talk about the battles of the Civil War was one of my first intellectual delights. I have always been suspicious of the dividing up of schools into grades, where one little soul knows no more and no less than any other little soul. The graded school is just a borrowing from the German *Volk-*

schule, anyhow. Now, the plan of using graduate student-teachers of which I spoke presents almost the only instance I know of in which undergraduate students have the advantage of being taught by teachers who are themselves actually studying. The results in intellectual comradeship and mutual sympathy are, so far as I can see, excellent.

Concerning the graduate college controversy I have little to contribute, especially since I am not in the least degree preparing a history of the university. I know the controversy was fraught with important, and also noisy, issues, but it left me cold. I had graduate training at Princeton before the later issues were born. As I have explained, we had an infant German system that was honorably and correctly followed. My degree, which I still consider respectable, was taken under Wilson's conditions, and I naturally sided with him. Further, Wilson's idea of placing the graduate college in the center of Princeton life, because it aimed towards unity of effort and association, seemed to me preferable to any sort of isolation, for I have always been against the American habit of splitting everything up into sections and specialties.

So far as I know—and, indeed, I am not an authority—the results of making the graduate college a separate entity have not been so socially segregative as it was feared they would be. I have visited the graduate college two or three times, in a strictly private capacity, and have met well-mannered and studious young men. I saw nothing that was snooty or monastic. The young men seemed to be going about their business in a business-like way. It is just possible, although it is a good deal to expect of modern young men, that graduate students actually walk from the college to the library, a distance, let us say, of two thousand yards. The graduate college did not seem to me "the geographical and spiritual center of the University," but it impressed me as a magnificent residential hall for a great institution of learning. Perhaps my own associations with members of the classes of 1899 and 1900 were closer than those of Princeton graduate students now, but there cannot be a significant difference.

The fact that the graduate college controversy was tied in with Wilson's quad plan must be kept in mind. He had expected that in his residential colleges postgraduate students would be included. With the defeat of that proposal, the possibility was lost. The idea is most attractive, but I do not know of any university in the United States where such a plan has even been tried. Wilson held fast to it, and the concept of the general association of faculty with all levels of the student body was also deeply entrenched in his mind. It is Wilson's ideas and not the events and debates at Princeton that are important in American higher education, and the notion of unified association in the presence of the job, widely used in business, is well worth the consideration of those in charge of universities and colleges. These institutions suffer from a diffusion of influence and energy because of their self-imposed classifications and barriers.

A statement of Wilson's position, now familiar to us, and his conception of the origin of the controversy is to be found in a letter that he prepared as an answer to a statement by former President Cleveland. Neither document was ever circulated, although Ray Stannard Baker published Wilson's statement as an appendix to the second volume of *Woodrow Wilson: Life and Letters.* It may make the issue clearer to quote a relevant part of the statement:

I can perhaps indicate in a few sentences the things that were in debate,—though the debate itself would be a very complicated thread to trace. Professor Andrew F. West, Dean of the Graduate School at Princeton, many years ago worked out a plan for a beautifully appointed house of residence for the fellows and some of the graduate students of the University, of which, as he then conceived it, we all thought well. It was to be placed at the geographical heart of the University, in close neighborhood to the libraries and laboratories, where the work of the men in residence might tell in all its seriousness upon the general life of the University, only too apt to be ignorant of the claims and interest of real scholarship and the scholarly life. But, as years went by, and the time approached when it was thought his plan might be put into operation, it greatly changed in his own mind, and lost all promise of its general use and effect upon the University. He wished his "Graduate College," which was in fact only to be an elaborate hall of residence, to be surrounded by gardens,—set off at a distance from the rest of the University, in order that its residents might be secluded to a life of their own, separated from the rest of the graduate students of the University as well as from the undergraduates, whose ideals their example had been intended to affect,— away from the libraries and laboratories, where it would be nothing but a beautiful place of retreat. I, for one, could not support such a plan.

A little farther on, two sentences connect this statement with the issue of club *vs.* residential college life, about which I have little more to say except that, for the mass of ordinary American students in universities and colleges—men glad enough to be there, busy in their own affairs and not often sensitive to ideas—Wilson's principles seem defeated:

During those same years the movement of college life at Princeton (naturally one of the most democratic of colleges) away from democracy to club life developed very rapidly, indeed. As President of the University, I met it and felt it at every turn. I found myself obliged to fight for a return to democracy all along the line, or else know that the young men in the University were not being properly prepared for American life or imbibing American ideals.[6]

6 *Life and Letters,* II, 358.

In point of fact, there was very little in the debate that concerned the nature and function of postgraduate study in American universities. It had to do with the legal aspects of the use of the Swann bequest at Princeton and with the question of whether the trustees under Wilson's leadership were justified in rejecting the Procter gift on the ground that it infringed on the freedom of the university by its dictation of educational policy. So far as I know, Wilson made few public utterances that had a bearing on graduate study.

Let it not be thought that Wilson gave up the fight over graduate study after the defeat of his plan for the reorganization of the social life of Princeton students. No doubt the year 1907–1908 was a bitter year for him, but, when he came back in the autumn of 1908, Princeton became about the liveliest place in the United States—rancorous, controversial, and mortifying. As I recall it, the undergraduates were only slightly affected, if at all. But the newspapers were full of it. Heated pamphlets were in circulation, and the *Alumni Weekly,* as well as various other journals, was jammed with letters—letters of protest, accusation, outright defense and rebuttal, and deprecation of the whole business. The points advanced really did not concern university life and learning. Partisanship and poorly informed controversy never produce sanity and truth. I seem to recall that the major figures in the controversy maintained their dignity, refrained from personalities, and remembered their responsibility to Princeton. Strange to say, the controversy ended in at least a temporary victory for Wilson. He had in his favor a majority of the trustees and a large majority of the alumni, and, as far as I could tell, the support of the student body. As to the faculty, I could count Wilson's outright enemies on my fingers; they were so few that, in numbers, at least, they did not amount to anything.

A question has, however, been raised from time to time

with reference to the attitude of the faculty towards Wilson's proposal for the reorganization of the social life of the student body. The faculty minutes make this matter perfectly clear. On September 26, 1907, a resolution was introduced by Daniels and seconded by Hunt:

Be it resolved that in the principle of the plan recently sanctioned by the Board of Trustees for the social co-ordination of the University, this Faculty do concur and that a committee of seven from this body be appointed to co-operate with the President of the University, the Dean of the Faculty, and the Committee of the Board of Trustees already constituted, to elaborate the plan in question.

Following this a substitute resolution was made by H. van Dyke and seconded by Hibben and McClenahan:

Resolved that we respectfully ask the Board of Trustees of the University that a representative joint Committee be appointed from their Honorable Body and from the Faculty which together with the President of the University shall investigate the present social condition of the University in conjunction with the representatives of the alumni and students and consider the best method of curing the evils which exist and of maintaining and promoting the unity, democracy, and scholarly life of the undergraduate body.

The pending resolution was debated at a meeting on September 30, 1907, and a vote was recorded by names on the substitute resolution, which took precedence over the original. Twenty-three voted for the substitute and eighty against it. The minutes of a meeting on October 7 contain a summary of Wilson's conception of the principles of the plan, listed as follows:

1. A new unit of organization.

2. Containing representatively all the elements of the University, the Faculty, and all the four classes of undergraduates.
3. Having a common life and an organization of its own, and
4. With a membership determined by some authority representing the University as a whole.

As stated, the plan was completely objective and had no trace of social reform. That is, it seemed to be a natural and reliable method of organization.

At a meeting on October 21, the president made known to the faculty the action of the board of trustees in reconsidering their earlier action endorsing the proposed plan and asking the president to withdraw it, and said that the plan had been withdrawn. Daniels' motion was then withdrawn by general consent.

Wilson's address before the Princeton Club of New York on January 10, 1910, presents his views on the location of the Princeton graduate college. It is perhaps the clearest and most closely reasoned of all his academic addresses. Its sole reliance is characteristically on an appeal to reason, and it is so important in understanding Wilson's ultimate beliefs that it deserves consideration here. It begins with a discussion of the rejection of the Procter gift, but does not describe it as an infringement on the right of Princeton to determine its own academic policies. It argues the matter on educational principles. Princeton must first acquire graduate students, and the plan proposed is too costly, since graduate students are professional students, who often have small means but are of the quality that Princeton wants. Conditions for graduate study must be economically practical at Princeton, which is at an experimental stage in its development. Graduate students are not looking for softer ways of living. He next argues the necessity of the integration of Princeton:

Undergraduates and graduates are facing acquaintance with one another, and the undergraduate is making a great discovery. He is making the discovery that interesting men, vital men, are engaged upon investigations the significance of which and the attractiveness of which he had never dreamed of.

And the benefit is not all on one side. The graduate is learning what inflammable matter, what delightful human subject-matter, he may have to deal with when he himself comes to instruct undergraduates.

Wilson closes with an argument of great power, the sort of thing that would free the imagination and appeal to the ideals of Princeton men:

Divorce the universities of this country from other lasting enthusiasms, divorce them from their undergraduates' energies, and you will have a thing which is not only un-American but utterly unserviceable to the country. There is nothing private in America. Everything is public; everything belongs to the united energy of the nation. . . . We must not be afraid of publicity; for the tribunal which is to judge Princeton does not sit in this room; it does not sit in any room where Princeton men are gathered; it does not sit in any room where a single class or body of men is gathered. The tribunal by which this university is to be judged is the nation itself. The voice of the nation will prevail to make her great, or to cover her with oblivion.

In the address there is also an argument for progress and development that ties the graduate school in with Wilson's conception of university education. It was, he says, the mission of President Eliot of Harvard to set the intellectual world free. Princeton must preserve that freedom and do so in such a way that it will be a generous freedom. Princeton has tried to do this by means of a constructive program. It has more to do. It must proceed constructively with its graduate program, which has not been of a character to achieve success. The learned world and the prospective graduate student are looking askance at Princeton, which must now act wisely and practically. Undergraduate students are not turning to intellectual pursuits, because they lack the impulse of advanced study and largely because they are not brought into contact with graduates.[7]

The political issues back of the graduate college controversy at Princeton I am neither willing nor able to discuss. I hope I have made it clear that, with reference to the educational and social issues already mentioned, I was and am in agreement with Wilson; nevertheless, I see no justice in the least misrepresentation of West's opinions and beliefs.

What puzzles me in my later years is why the controversy ever came to a head. There seem to me many more areas of agreement than of difference between Wilson and West. There is hardly a principal statement in West's great article, "The Proposed Graduate College of Princeton," that Wilson would not have endorsed. Indeed, the two men were for years intimate friends who agreed in their academic philosophy. Both conceived of universities as servants of the state and of human culture and betterment. Both were pupils of McCosh and sought to follow the road marked out by him, that is, to arrive at truth by means of broad knowledge and the guidance of enlightened intuition, and the only divergence in fundamental principles I can see is that Wilson believed in a general body—the graduate school—as an active and integrated part of the university operating in behalf of learned culture within it, while West believed in

[7] *Princeton Alumni Weekly,* Vol. X (1909–10), 447–53.

proceeding by segregation of the best students. West's view, except in politics, is not necessarily aristocratic. Both views are now held by competent men in the field of education.

Both Wilson and West were essentially reformers, and the necessity of reform is still with us. I have come to believe in the vast possibility of all human minds and am afraid to be too hastily selective, since the criteria of selection seem to me imperfect. I therefore lean strongly to Wilson's side.

Dean West was a classicist and a convincing defender of the classics in education. He hated to see the fulfillment of McCosh's prophecy: "If our colleges discard Latin and Greek, the whole ancient world with its thoughts and deeds will remain very much unknown even to our educated men." West, too, was a pupil of McCosh, and this means that he opposed, as I do, the narrowing of American higher education by utilitarian ends and overspecialization. He sought from a most elevated station the triumph of the best that has been known and thought in the world. He probably did alter his stand, as Wilson said he did, in regard to the relation of the proposed graduate college to the university as a whole, but that change was not necessarily due to undemocratic principles. It seems more probable that he came to believe, consciously or unconsciously, that the selection of the best students was the more feasible, even natural, road to the improvement of American culture. He talked to me at length on the occasion of a visit he made to Minneapolis after I had gone to the University of Minnesota. He explained his position and in his picturesque manner scouted the idea that he did not adhere to the very essence of American democracy. He professed disquietude of mind lest through misinformation the ancient democracy of Princeton should be impeached. Let us follow his reasoning as he expresses it in the article referred to above, subtitled "With Some Reflections on the Humanizing of Learning":

144

Like civil liberty, the higher liberal knowledge is always in peril and always worth fighting for. Just now it is facing the perils of deterioration and dismemberment. Among the forces that threaten it, the commercial spirit is probably the strongest. It means the pursuit of only such knowledge as "pays," the absorption in material ends, the rating of a living as higher than a life. This spirit, not satisfied with engrossing the business life of the country and at times menacing its political integrity, seeks to affect every part of our education. Its attack is made on the foundations. Whenever it enters side by side with purely liberal studies in the college course it starts to drive them out or else forces them to be taught in a utilitarian way, practically giving them the alternative of deterioration to escape extinction. The truth that all high-minded knowledge is in the best sense useful, is torn and twisted into the half-truth of "service," the doctrine that only the knowledge of obvious use is worth having.

Another threatening force is unenlightened specialization. It breaks the structure of higher knowledge into fragments. That the scholar should be in some important sense a specialist is true. That he should be only a specialist is a calamity to himself and others. True specialization has its indispensable value in the exact determination of particulars and in accurately relating particulars to the general. But the man who is only a specialist is but a fraction. A preliminary sound training in liberal studies is the best guarantee we have that the intending scholar of good native capacities is likely to be whole-minded, that he will be a citizen not only of the place where his special work lies, but of the commonwealth of knowledge. What has been happening these twenty years or more? Erratic men of mediocre or inferior powers have been flocking into their specialties. What liberal training they may have had has been weakened by disuse. They have intensive knowledge of one thing, which is very well indeed, with extensive ignorance of most other things, which is not well at all.

Still another untoward result follows. The fractionally-minded scholar is not naturally capable, or at least is not easily capable of whole-minded judgments, which are the only ones fundamentally sound. If, as Huxley said, scientific insight is nothing more than "highly trained common sense" applied to scientific questions, then highly trained common sense—just another name for sound judgment, is the one thing needful to all sensible scholarship. Good sense naturally goes with large vision. The man who has taken a sweeping view around the horizon is the one best able to discern the place and size of one or another segment of the scene, and the scholar already trained in studies of universal value is the one who can be depended on most surely to possess the wide-ranging well-balanced view.[8]

This same philosophy, in which West and Wilson concur, can be found in the writings of Ormond and other Princeton men of those days. It was at that time a tower of strength to Princeton, and has now come back into vogue equipped with a new logic and a new theory of cognition. I see no reason why, with its history of great things done and attempted by Woodrow Wilson, Princeton should not recognize an impulsive unity in its thought larger than partisanship or self-adulation.

[8] *Century,* Vol. 81 (February, 1911), 600–612.

CHAPTER VI

Opportunity and Vision

An evidence not only of Wilson's genius but of his continued importance as an authority on education comes from his discovery and adoption of at least two fundamental principles concerning the development of the individual human being. These principles, although now well known, have not had the recognition they deserve in the field of higher education. His identification and adoption of them are the more remarkable because he seems to have arrived at them without any greatly particularized study of philosophy and psychology.

The first of these is the discovery of what is today recognized as the very essence of mental growth. It is what is now called symbolization. Many of the more advanced thinkers about education of our time see in this process of learning not only the characteristic feature of definitely human mentality as distinguished from that of other animals but the fundamentals of the art of thinking and understanding. Adam, we are told, gave names to all the creatures in Paradise, and that is what the learning child and adult human creature do as their minds grow. Wilson perceived this principle early in life, adhered to it as he grew older, and finally made it the basis of his attempt to reform the system of university teaching. He could not have been more nearly right. He called it "discussion," "comradeship in learning," and the "laying of minds side by side," for his terminology was of the simplest. He saw the high road to truth in the process of sharing and testing, for symbols, especially language, depend on consent and are social, not individual. It is the same process as that which makes children ask questions and handle objects.

Wilson laid great stress on his intellectual association with his friends in college and seems to have been very fortunate in the quality of the men who made up his group. This intercourse was for him a major experience, and he believed in it as such throughout his career. His association with his friends, his readiness to debate, his habit of careful, critical listening, his faith in the enlightened opinions of humanity, and his willingness to accept advice on doubtful issues may all be described as acts in the great human drama of symbolization. The idea need not rest on the technical meaning of the word, for that meaning is merely observation, recognition, discrimination, and thought or reflection leading to the determination of truth of both fact and principle. To Wilson, it was the zest of youth manifesting itself in congenial and untrammeled surroundings in the process of education. This is the idea that made its appearance in the American university world as the preceptorial system.

To what extent this fundamental procedure is followed in American university teaching would be difficult to determine. I have reason to think, on the basis of my own experience, that there is little conscious practice of it and little knowledge even of the existence of the principle. My colleagues have nearly all been specialists. In point of fact, symbolization is a natural, even an essential, method of education, for teaching can be good only in proportion to its symbolical efficiency. The great foundations now engaged in setting American higher education to rights do not know this, but it is nevertheless true. This method of communication, criticism, and exchange of ideas, with adjustment of environment in varying degrees, as Wilson would have had it adjusted, must be widely, although often unconsciously used; thus in these cases the only question is an old one: If University teachers knew what they were doing, would they do it better?

As to Princeton, I am unfortunately not well informed. I found, however, a clear indication of the course charted by the faculty, which I think is worthy of inclusion here. In the autumn of 1910, after Wilson's resignation of the presidency of Princeton, the faculty ordered the appointment of a committee to draft a resolution appropriate to the occasion. The committee included Professors Ormond, Abbott, Daniels, Hunt, and W. F. Magie. This resolution was presented and adopted at a meeting on November 21. It was carefully drafted and carefully written. It states that for many years Wilson had been an "esteemed and distinguished member of the academic body." He had been confronted with vital questions of university policy and met them with the institution of a departmental system in the election of courses, which is described as a solution of the problem of freedom in the choice of courses; and also with the institution of the preceptorial system, which was a preservation of individual instruction along with the creation of closer and less formal relations between students and instructors. The resolution then states:

He was convinced that forces were at work that were inconsistent with the spirit of equality on which Princeton has always laid so much stress, and though the only measure which was proposed as a remedy gave rise to violent controversy, it will be readily acknowledged that Dr. Wilson has by his powerful appeals aroused the attention of the academic world to the existence of certain tendencies in the social life of our Colleges and Universities which demand the most serious consideration.

Attention is called to Wilson's achievements in the growth and strengthening of the institution, to material growth, to the development of the sciences, and the observation is made most interestingly that material growth has been paralleled by intellectual growth. The intellectual standards of the student body have been raised. Princeton has grown in national importance and public esteem and has been kept in close touch and sympathy with the broader life of the nation. Finally, the resolution speaks generously and proudly of Wilson's entrance into public life. Princeton has been the mother of statesmen: "The laurels he wins will be ours also."

The resolution is a complete endorsement of Wilson's educational principles, and, as is the reticent habit of faculties, an adoption of those principles. The Princeton faculty stood firm in the years that followed, and I think still stands firm, in its support of the standards and principles it instituted and adopted during the years of my service. Whatever diversion and changes there may have been in succeeding years, the Princeton faculty to its everlasting credit has given no ground in essential matters.

Wilson's reply is dated December 3 and was read to the faculty but not transcribed in the minutes. It is brief, but I think there is no doubt that Wilson fulfilled his purpose in the message: "It is one of the happiest circumstances of my life that I should have won the confidence and admiration of such a body of men, and it will certainly aid me constantly in the performance of the duties that lie ahead of me to know that their expectations follow me with confidence and affection."[1]

The second of Wilson's great educational principles, mainly adopted from his philosophical inheritance reinforced by the teachings of McCosh and Princeton, may be described as the natural epistemology of enlightened and enlightening humanity. Wilson's perception of this theory of learning was clear, but found no statement theoretically or philosophically. As we have seen, the method was definitely put into practice during Wilson's experience as a graduate student at the Johns Hopkins University. It appears also in many of his informal comments on his own experience as student and scholar. This epistemology underlay Wilson's curricular reform at Princeton, although there it did not come to full expression and adoption. It is the theory of the completest possible knowledge leading to the achievement of the fullest possible comprehension, which in turn leads to an immediate perception of truth. It appeared, as we have seen, most clearly in Wilson's own scholarly work, in his habit of thoroughness and exactitude in investigation, and in his habit of thought.

It was manifest, although not so fully as one could wish, in the arrangement of the course of study at Princeton, for a severer application might have resulted in making a distinction between those subjects of study, such as the natural sciences, that gain by the use of a deductive method and rely for the proof of their findings on experiment and argument, and the discursive branches of learning—the humanities, the social sciences, religion, and philosophy itself—that must, since experiment is limited, proceed inductively. The inductive point of view demands breadth of knowledge, including knowledge of the interrelations of subjects, and, although Wilson effected a natural and most beneficial union among history, politics, and economics, departmental separations and rivalries prevented such unions in other areas

1 Woodrow Wilson Collection, Princeton University Library.

where it is most desirable. This educationally important principle in the approach to discursive studies has rarely if ever been recognized in American university education. The result, as one can see, is very great confusion, a most unfortunate splitting apart of disciplines closely related to one another, indeed, actually interdependent, and a consequent narrowing of the training of university teachers in these related fields and probably in the sciences themselves, for the deep chasm between natural sciences and the discursive subjects is, from the point of view of university function, most unfortunate.

Wilson's recognition of the necessity of an *a posteriori* approach to discursive subjects was personal and tentative, although unmistakably anticipatory of the farthest advance of the philosophy of learning in our modern world. Here, in my judgment and from the point of view of my own subject, lies the greatest necessity for extensive and difficult reform before the university world at this time. Politics grows more and more confused, economics, at a time of great financial inflation, has nothing significant to contribute, and literature is a hopeless jumble of ill-formed and inconsistent classes and operates according to a metaphysics which is false and special to itself; but, if anybody thinks such a reform is easy to bring about, let him try it for himself. The world of the discursive subjects is full of unwarranted commitments, vested interests, and ineffectual doctrines—all tightly adhered to.

Wilson encountered barriers in the application of his two great ideas to the problems of university education. As to the first, the natural exercise of the process of learning, he was keenly aware of the limitations and hindrances in the way of its operation to be found in university instruction. There was a stiffness and pomposity in the professorial attitude which has now no doubt greatly abated or changed to indifference. As to the diversion of student interest by extra-curricular activities, athletics, courtship, and social ambition, what the educator of today meets is probably much more powerful than anything Wilson encountered at Princeton. He saw that the success of his teaching method depended on ease and freedom, since the effectual operation of it is spontaneous and not compulsive. He observed the lack of this freedom in the formal use of lectures and tests with their artificial remoteness of teacher from pupil. He found no meeting of minds in the use of the lecture system as a sole reliance. There was utility in lectures, but Wilson wanted to make sure that the student reacted within himself to the facts and ideas presented. His desire for this response often took the form of dislike of dogmatism, pedantry, egotism, and anything else that might stand in the way of a union between the operations of teaching and learning. He believed there should be no barrier between the student and the area where truth is to be found. He therefore disliked any sort of rote learning or authoritative control. He saw quite clearly that lack of personal acquaintance between teacher and pupil was an initial barrier, and in the face of this difficulty he invented a system by means of which students would be associated with preceptors for long periods in the pursuit and comprehension of fields of learning. Such teaching is both desirable and practical and would be effective, but, with most American universities already understaffed, there is not much that can be done about it.

Wilson, in adhering to his belief in learning rather than teaching, did not reject the teaching function of universities, but sought to change its operation so that the teacher became not so much an instrument for instruction as for assistance. Certainly this was a move in the right direction. His attempt to establish this altered function as the general practice was very successful at Princeton, where it narrowed the gap between university students and teachers and brought about a rise in the intellectual level of the student body. There has certainly appeared since Wilson's time a closer relationship between these constituent classes. I think that his spirit and ideals have been potent. But I shall not be satisfied until the emphasis in higher education is definitely shifted from teaching to learning.

Wilson's epistemology is particularly applicable to the vast fields that he called "reading subjects." This application seems to me of special importance, since it affects the course of study itself as well as methodology. It is important that universities recognize the natural division of the *studium generale* into discursive and scientific subjects and consciously adapt their views and methods to the situation. The elements of such an adaptation cannot be detailed offhand, since the thought and experience of many men would be required to work out the order of procedure. The chief obstacle to such reform seems to be the attitudes of university teachers themselves and their adherence to conventional methods, including extreme specialization. Whether the university teachers of this generation will awaken to the significance of our age is open to question, but I feel sure that the new findings of scientists and philosophers will eventually have their way.

The approach to human culture in the modern university has been made too difficult. The effect of the best modern thought is to make it simpler and in line with nature. This complication has come about largely from the borrowing and enforcement of a largely inapplicable method to fields of learning in which it did not and could not apply. The method is wrong. Here, again, learning is more important than teaching; that is, the scholar should have control of his subject, and truth should come to him as a result of comprehension. He should not search for truth in a discursive field by means of theories, hypotheses, and conjectures. This has been the erroneous platform for the investigation of questions that arise in the humanities, the social sciences, religion, and all branches of philosophy. Wilson's recommendation is therefore a natural one, age old and long known: the completest possible knowledge and a love of truth that will not be satisfied with anything else, plus the sanest possible mind.

Commentaries that contribute any understanding to a study of American universities from the point of view of Wilson's principles of education are few. Such studies as exist—for example, in the bulletins of the American Association of University Professors, the publications of the General Education Board, and the Carnegie Foundation for the Advancement of Teaching—do contain a certain amount of relevant matter, but it is scattered and casual. The prevailing interests of these and other associations are finance, government, and other strictly professional matters. A few books have been published on university education, and I have examined with interest A. Lawrence Lowell's *At War with Academic America* (1934), Guy Stanton Ford's *On and Off the Campus* (1938), and a book with a promising title, *The Obligations of Universities to the Social Order* (1933), edited by N. Edwards and H. G. Richey. The last contains about sixty brief articles written mainly by educators and educational administrators and presents some interesting material in all too abbreviated and disconnected form. Since most other publications I have found are at best only vaguely applicable to my subject, I must make my limited contribution without their help.

There can be no doubt that the eyes of the university world were on Princeton during Wilson's administration, that great hope was aroused by his reforms, and that his tremendous popularity persisted unbroken for a decade after he left Princeton. In addition, student-faculty relations were markedly closer and less formal in all universities after World War I. One cannot, of course, attribute this closer association to the influence of Wilson or Princeton. The causes were national, even international, and cannot be readily identified and assessed. The war certainly gave formalism of various sorts a rough jolt; universities possibly lost some authority over their students; communication became rapid and more extended; and there were various agencies that had liberalizing, specializing, and disruptive influences on universities.

However, Princeton was a great institution, and Wilson's reforms were widely known among educators. Further, many Princeton men of the early 1900's later taught in various universities, and members of Wilson's faculty moved to other schools, and we may be reasonably sure that they carried with them Princeton ideals and attitudes. That they did so is evident in Edgar Odell Lovett's organization of Rice Institute and, I have been told, in the administration of Harry A. Garfield at Williams College. I mention only two, but there were others. Frank Aydelotte's more Oxford-like experiment at Swarthmore College stemmed from a similar philosophy, and Yale and Harvard were possibly influenced by Wilson's efforts when they made provision for the promotion of student-faculty association. Although I think it likely, I do not insist that American universities have been influenced by Wilson and Princeton, because I know that some American universities think of themselves as creations *de novo* and are reluctant to acknowledge obligation or influence.

American universities face a still more difficult problem— that of making their purposes and ideals crystal clear to their own faculties and students and to the general public as well. The American university, by and large, is an autocracy and has no public voice except that of its president, and, indeed, no internal voice except his. This is frequently the case even when the university is not autocratic in practice. Deans and department heads as a rule speak only for their special domains and have little to say to the university as a whole or to the university world. As a result the ordinary faculty member and student do not know what the university stands for and what it would like to accomplish educationally. Ideals and purposes are seldom discussed with young instructors, who could be of great assistance in spreading knowledge of them through their contacts with students. True, freshmen usually undergo an orientation period during which such topics are mentioned, but since they are newly arrived and still bewildered, they do not readily retain the information. It seems to me, therefore, that one of the great needs in higher education today is to implant firmly in the minds of students and faculty the goals, aims, ambitions—whatever you want to call these larger purposes—of the institution. Of course, even the most brilliant, the most dedicated university president cannot do everything, but I think that he ought to find time to follow Wilson's example in making ideals clear, and large enrollments are no excuse for failure to do so.

The very heart of Wilson's doctrine was his deep conviction that it was not only a primary responsibility of universities to serve the state but a reason for their existence. His own special subject was the science of government, which by its very nature put special emphasis on the training of university students to be good citizens and honest and faithful servants of the people through public office. To understand his view fully, one must recognize Wilson's own intense and intelligent patriotism. To him, the foundation of the American republic was prepared for through the ages and made possible by the wisdom, courage, and moral force of generations of British and American people. It was not a casual or accidental invention but the very destiny of our people.

Wilson did not stop with teaching political rectitude and the restoration of the liberty-loving statesmanship of our forefathers. His morality pervaded his whole being and was alert to every issue that appeared, so that it is impossible to draw a hard-and-fast line between politics and morality as they appeared in his thought. But no discussion of Wilson's moral character can provide the illumination that comes from many a paragraph in his writings, for example, the following from "Abraham Lincoln: A Man of the People," an address delivered at Chicago on the one hundredth anniversary of Lincoln's birth, February 12, 1909:

And then, last and greatest characteristic of all, a man of the people is a man who has felt that unspoken, that intense, that almost terrifying struggle of humanity, that struggle whose object is, not to get forms of government, not to realize particular formulas or make for any definite goal, but simply to live and be free. He has participated in that struggle; he has felt the blood stream against the tissue; he has known anxiety; he has felt that life contained for him nothing but effort, effort from the rising of the sun to the going down of it. He has, therefore, felt beat in him, if he had any heart, a universal sympathy for those who struggle, a universal understanding of the unutterable things that were in their hearts and the unbearable burdens that were upon their backs. . . . [Lincoln's] was part of the toil; he had part and lot in the struggle; he knew the uncertainty of the goal mankind had but just touched and from which they had been [beaten] back; knew that the price of life is blood, and that no man who goes jauntily and complacently through the world will ever touch the springs of human action. Such a man with such a consciousness, such a universal human sympathy, such a universal comprehension of what life means, is your man of the people, and no one else can be.

But this is not the complete expression of Wilson. There

must also be included his drive for action as the consequence of an act of clear cognition, as expressed a little farther on in the same address:

What shall we do? . . . We live, and we have no other choice, in this age, and the tasks of this age are the only tasks to which we are asked to address ourselves. We are not asked to apply our belated wisdom to the problems and perplexities of an age that is gone. We must have timely remedies suitable for the existing moment. If that be true, the only way in which we can worthily celebrate a great man is by showing today that we have not lost the tradition of force which made former ages great, that we can produce them continuously in a kind of our own.[2]

My point here is that Wilson believed that universities ought to serve the state, and that by this phrase he meant the service of mankind, very like what our religious forefathers called the service of God. Our present-day intense individualism, which in my judgment is three parts selfishness, may prompt us to retort that many universities are private corporations owing no funds or support to the government and therefore at liberty to teach what they please and pursue such purposes as they may choose. But Wilson thought not, and believed so strongly in this purpose that he made it the text of his first address of truly national scope, "Princeton in the Nation's Service," delivered on October 21, 1896. There was no great novelty in such a profession of patriotic good will. The novelty was that Wilson meant it, repeated it again and again, made every effort to carry it out at Princeton, and, it may be, wrecked his university career in his attempt to prevent Princeton from practicing what he regarded as social injustice.

Indeed, most of Wilson's educational principles were de-

[2] *Public Papers*, II, 83–101.

rived from, or concomitant with, his belief in the responsibility of universities to the general welfare. I think the idea is sound and true, that it was much needed in his time, and that the principle is a natural and proper one for all Americans to embrace. I think it applies to every individual, corporation, or association that lives and carries on its business on the soil of the American republic. Is it, after all, too much to expect, as Wilson did, that citizens should pay for their privileges by loyalty to our country and responsibility to the community?

Wilson believed in liberty under the law, and what he did and said about it deserves close attention. I recall, for example, the strong impression he made upon me when, in discussing the device employed by the predatory rich of having their hirelings do their dirty work, he said, "Let the law punish these malefactors one after another according to their deserts, and it will soon come about that these sheltered criminals will no longer be able to hire such agents." It seems to me, in any case, perfectly possible to generalize Wilson's doctrine of the public responsibilities of universities and to find it sound and applicable all the way through.

As far as the current situation is concerned, I rather think that the principle of university responsibility to the state belongs to that large and rather hopeless class of duties the validity of which everybody admits and almost nobody attends to. In my long career as a university teacher I have seen very little stress placed on the subject. Most universities fly the Stars and Stripes as a matter of routine. Some require a faculty member to sign an oath of allegiance before a notary before he can be paid. Laws have been passed in many states requiring students in state-supported schools to complete a minimum number of courses in American history and government—and unfortunately the courses can often be described as "minimum," too. But these things represent mere lip-service or formal compliance with law. When they are compared with Wilson's deep sincerity in his pride of country and solicitude for its welfare, the total ascertainable activity of universities is not impressive.

Most present-day universities teach morality and good behavior to their students by the somewhat dubious method of attempting to catch and punish offenders. Conscious or deliberate efforts to teach morality are usually in the hands of deans of men and women and other advisers. This is their business, and they no doubt do it well, although they might perhaps do it better if they had more support from faculties. The baleful spectre of specialization casts its shadow here, too. Faculty members teach their own subjects, work at their own problems, and turn morals over to those who are paid to uphold them. Wilson believed that moral principles were achieved through the building of character, which is a higher level of ethics, and it may well be that he has many worthy and effective followers on university staffs who hold the same view and achieve the same results. Let us hope so.

Another ideal of university achievement closely connected with morality and ethics is sustaining and improving the intellectual level of the student body. McCosh worked at this directly and avowedly at Princeton, and so did Wilson. Attention to the intellectual level is a primary duty and function of college and university presidents, who often think they are too busy to take direct action, and often neglect it or entrust it solely to others. The intellectual development of the Princeton student body was a principal concern to Wilson and his colleagues, who thought it the reason for the existence of universities. With this end in view, Wilson rebuilt his faculty and engineered the construction of a course of study which was designed to be not only useful and workable but challenging and interesting. I think he succeeded as no other educator in my experience has done.

The subtleties of Wilson's educational thought, especially in its larger integrations, are not easy to comprehend; for example, his belief in human liberty as an all-important moral and social force. Manifest throughout his writings, it is phrased particularly well in a compilation from Wilson's speeches during his first campaign for the presidency, entitled *The New Freedom: A Call for the Emancipation of the Generous Energies of a People* (1913). It echoes with the principles of Wilson's Princeton career and almost mystically exalts liberty and its power to correct evil and establish good. This is a new age, it declares; progress may be slow, but it is real; free men need no guardians; life comes from the soil; justice is a right, not a benevolence; "the way to resume is to resume," that is the American way; business needs and will welcome emancipation from its own selfish sins; and the liberation of the energies of the people, the greatest need, will result from complete manumission:

We have got to cheer and inspirit our people with the sure prospects of social justice and due reward, with the vision of the open gates of opportunity for all. We have got to let the energy and the initiative of this great people go absolutely free, so that the future of America will be greater than the past, so that the pride of America will grow with achievement, so that America will know as she advances from generation to generation that each brood of her sons is greater and more enlightened than that which preceded it, know that she is fulfilling the promise she has made to mankind. . . . [Liberty] has not ceased to be a fundamental demand of the human spirit, a fundamental necessity for the life of the soul.[3]

Wilson was no mystic, but had formed a broad conception

[3] These addresses have appeared in a fuller version in *A Crossroads to Freedom* (New Haven, 1956).

of the nature and function of liberty. I, for one, should like to know more about the genesis, the bases, and the interconnections of this great force in the successful life of a completely free humanity—free from fear and want, from superstition and ignorance, from dogma and intolerance, and from the shackles of sensuality and selfishness.

Here is another instance in which Wilson anticipated the latest philosophy of our time. The doctrine of the effect of hindrance and frustration of the human spirit and the consequence of the emancipation of the "generous energies" of men is recurrent in the philosophy of A. N. Whitehead. Note, for example, the following passage from *Adventures of Ideas:*

The concept of freedom has been narrowed to the picture of contemplative people shocking their generation. When we think of freedom we are apt to confine ourselves to freedom of thought, freedom of the press, freedom for religious opinions. Then the limitations to freedom are conceived as wholly arising from the antagonism of our fellow men. This is a thorough mistake. The massive habits of physical nature, its iron laws, determine the scene for the sufferings of men. Birth and death, heat, cold, hunger, separation, disease, the general impracticability of purpose, all bring their quota to imprison the souls of women and of men. Our experiences do not keep step with our hopes. The Platonic Eros, which is the soul stirring itself to life and motion, is maimed. The essence of freedom is the practicability of purpose.[4]

The above passage is quoted in *Philosophy in a New Key,* by Susanne Langer, who relates Whitehead's idea to the spiritually shackled condition of ordinary men in the modern world:

The mind, like all other organs, can draw its sustenance only

4 (New York, 1933), 84.

from the surrounding world; our metaphysical symbols must spring from reality. Such adaptation always requires time, habit, tradition, and intimate knowledge of a way of life. If, now the field of our unconscious symbolic orientation is suddenly plowed up by tremendous changes in the external world and in the social order, we lose our hold, our convictions, and therewith our effectual purposes. In modern civilization there are two great threats to mental security: the new mode of living, which has made the old nature-symbols alien to our minds, and the new mode of working, which makes personal activity meaningless, inacceptable to the hungry imagination. Most men never see the goods they produce, but stand by a traveling belt and turn a million identical passing screws or close a million identical passing wrappers in a succession of hours, days, years. . . . The withdrawal of all natural means for expressing the unity of personal life is a major cause of the distraction, irreligion, and unrest that mark the proletariat of all countries. Technical progress is putting man's freedom of mind in jeopardy.[5]

And from Mrs. Langer's admirable statement comes the suggestion of another of Wilson's surprising anticipations of present-day thought, which concerns a matter of importance to university education—faith in the possibilities or capabilities of the individual. I have discussed this topic at length earlier, but it deserves mention in this summing up.

It was obvious in every move that Wilson made at Princeton, both as teacher and as administrator, that he not only wanted things done but believed they could be done. Aspiration and efficiency were blended in his make-up, and he preached the one and expected the other. He took it for granted that his pupils could achieve the high purposes he recommended. This certainly accounts for the generally acknowledged inspiration and encouragement he gave his

[5] (Cambridge, Mass., 1951), 291–92.

pupils and younger colleagues. He seems never to have doubted their ability to achieve great things, hard things.

On the basis of what is known about the structure and operation of the human brain, it is concluded that the possibilities of intellection are inconceivably great—three billion is the sum proposed for synaptic connections—and also that the extent to which such synaptic possibilities are normally realized is disappointingly small—something like one success in one thousand chances, which is a poor score in any game. Now, if university students have, as is reliably claimed, these vast possibilities, it seems to me that university teachers should be aware of them and should act accordingly, especially since selectivity has no bearing on the matter. Teachers might require more and expect more of their students and try for more distant and difficult goals with more hope of reaching them. They might even discover that extreme specialization is not necessary after all, and might increase the range as well as the intensity of learning. University teachers might then have something to work and hope for. A bare half-million new cognitive connections put into the heads of university graduates might transform our alumni.

This brings us back to a consideration of the fact that in American universities there is as yet no generally accepted principle of arranging a course of study. Neither of Wilson's two major contentions—that there is a logical and propaedeutic order in which subjects should be studied and that every department of a university should include matter pertaining to the general culture—is generally accepted. As has been seen, Wilson applied these principles to his reformation of the Princeton curriculum and extended them to technical and professional education, maintaining that no university should operate as a mere feeder of manufacturing, commerce, and the closed professions.

While Wilson's ideas of orderly procedure in study and

the necessity of general culture have not been summarily rejected, neither have they been as widely followed and as sincerely believed in as in a republic they ought to be. The evils of the free election of courses have by no means disappeared, and there is little chance that they will disappear. Almost the only unanimous faculty vote of which I have any knowledge, and that in a great university, was in favor of putting all courses and subjects on uniform display in class schedules and curriculum lists, the idea being that every department would thus get a share of student choices.

Small colleges still retain their advantages in regard to courses of study as well as in personal contact between teachers and students. Some of them are excellent both in curriculum and in teaching methods. Others seem to have surrendered to the modern social urge and function largely as rather inferior matrimonial agencies. Significantly, excellence is not a matter of wealth and prosperity, for some small colleges engaged in a life-and-death struggle for survival are sustained by their loyalty to good ends, and serve their students in admirable fashion. Small colleges may not fit their students to handle machines, sell goods, or manage credit buying, but they often contribute a substantial number of good citizens and enterprising Americans.

In any examination of the present-day American university, we must recognize the fact that all institutions of higher learning are menaced by the frivolities, the easy dishonesties, and the hard-shelled indifference of the current social order. However, in this effort to evaluate the American university in terms of Wilson's high and enduring educational principles, we have had also to acknowledge our own shortcomings as university teachers, at the same time remembering that most of these principles are old but have never established themselves effectively in universities, where one would think they would have the best chance to prevail. We have found the most fault with ourselves as university teachers, which is legitimate and ought not to be offensive. That some teachers are indifferent to the hopeful and useful findings of our own age and persist in following outworn, conventional lines of belief and action is cause for concern, but it must not be forgotten that universities are understaffed and professors ill paid and too often regarded as hired men. I shall not despair, however, when we acknowledge that part of the fault is our own.

Perhaps the story of the discouragement of the Old Testament prophet Elijah has some pertinence here. Elijah had slain the prophets of Baal by the brook of Kishan. When Ahab told Jezebel what Elijah had done, Jezebel threatened to "make thy life as the life of one of them." Thereupon Elijah fled a day's journey into the wilderness, where he sat down under a juniper tree and fell into great despondency. He asked the Lord to take his life because he was not better than his fathers. The angel of the Lord appeared to him and directed him to go to Mount Horeb, and there Elijah complained that the children of Israel had forsaken the covenant of the Lord, thrown down His altars, and slain His prophets with the sword, and "I, even I only, am left; and they seek my life to take it away." And the Lord replied, "Yet have I left me seven thousand in Israel, all the knees which have not bowed unto Baal, and every mouth which hath not kissed him." Then He gave Elijah three important tasks to carry out.

The Lord's reply to Elijah suggests my position regarding university reformation, for truth and righteousness do prevail day by day, whatever we in our blindness and self-conceit may think. I am solemnly convinced that the only important result universities can accomplish is the education of university students, which is largely an individual and unspectacular matter. I also believe that the United States has about as good institutions of higher learning as its culture and character entitle it to have. It follows that the only way to better the status of universities is to improve that culture and character.

Great leaders like Wilson have made heroic efforts in this direction, but great leaders are scarce, and those who dare to be ahead of their times are often penalized, as Wilson was. There is no doubt, however, that great principles have an immortality of their own. Because such principles are wise and true, they are subject to revival and to continued use by even the most obscure university teacher. Wilson believed in the perdurable nature of truth and in its efficacy. All teachers, whether or not concerned with the selection of administrators and the determination of policy, have full access to Wilson's teachings, teachings that concern them directly in the task that matters most.

Before this discussion of Wilson's educational principles and policies is closed, two additional expressions of his views, both made near the end of his formal career as an educator, deserve attention. The first is his brief address at the inauguration of H. A. Garfield as president of Williams College, October 7, 1908. Wilson had had and was still undergoing trying experiences, but his concept of what the nation needed from the learned world was ever clearer and more emphatic:

Men who can think, men who can interpret, men who can perceive, men who have something more than skill and aptitude and knowledge, men who look beneath the surface of affairs and know the genesis of affairs and can forecast . . . the future of affairs, . . . men whose attention is not wholly centred upon making their own living, but is spent also upon the very exigent matter of lifting all the counsels of the country to a higher plane and place and opportunity of vision.

I know of no more representative utterance of Wilson's

and none better worth heeding by schools and universities, but it was not his last word on the subject. In a very charming unpublished address made at Franklin and Marshall College on January 10, 1910, most of Wilson's characteristic ideas and principles are expressed in simple and comprehensible form. Although the essay was written in a troubled and controversial time, something about the friendly and hopeful occasion seems to have lifted his spirits, so that the address serves in slightly reminiscent fashion to interpret Wilson to those who labor in the vineyard.

In a humorous introduction, he speaks of the miscellaneous public duties of college and university presidents, but concludes that these officials are called on to give unprejudiced advice. In the same vein he says that it is the duty of colleges to make young gentlemen as unlike their fathers as possible, not out of prejudice against the fathers, but to correct the narrowness that these worthies suffer in each generation through business or special occupation, and to restore, in the region where the great trade winds of doctrine blow, a sane and intelligent attitude. The operation has become more and more difficult because of increasing worldly activities—sports, social engagements, amusements of various sorts—that leave for the colleges only a residuum of the student's attention. Society has invaded the college. College is not a place to pursue business—nothing but make-believe business prevails there. The situation now is such that universities must recapture the strategic positions that are necessary in order that they may be the real purveyors of knowledge. All history shows that the vital force comes from the bottom—men of culture may be the flowers of civilization, but "the plant has its roots in the dark processes of the silent earth." This statement he illustrates by a comparison of Benjamin Franklin and John Marshall, the eminent men for whom the college was named.

There follows a cento of Wilson's college and university ideals: Colleges and universities are engaged in a minor form of statesmanship. Knowledge is not education. Education consists in the establishment in the mind of certain habits and powers that are confirmed by use, by constant practice; it does not consist of accumulations of knowledge—"good information passing through the mind may leave no trace." The faculties of men must be released; there is great need of this in the presence of rapid change—"If the student has been taught only the process, he cannot adapt himself to change; but, if he is taught to use his mind upon any process, he can." Publicity is a legitimate part of public business—and universities and colleges are public business—for this openness is the way of reform. Let the people know what the actual facts about colleges are—not sensationally or by misrepresentation, but truthfully, so that parents may fear for the education of their sons and thus willingly co-operate in the removal of obstacles. Colleges are about to gain the whole world in numbers and lose their own souls by not providing an atmosphere in which the real communion of thought, the real academic spirit, can breathe. Whether this last statement of Wilson's was a prophecy or a timely warning, only the future can reveal.

Index

Woodrow Wilson at Princeton has been set in Baskerville, a very useful and highly readable type face. It has been said of Baskerville that "it is the connecting link between the age of tradition, which it brought to a close, and the age of revolution, which it ushered in."

University of Oklahoma Press : Norman